COSORI Smart Air Fryer Toaster Oven Combo Cookbook for Beginners

1000 Days of Crispy, Fresh & Healthy Air Fryer Oven Combo Recipes for Quick & Hassle-Free Meals - Anyone Can Cook

Jensson Raden

Table of Contents

Introduction

The Cosori smart air fryer toaster oven is one of the advanced and innovative cooking appliances manufactured by COSORI. It is a multi-functional 12 in 1 cooking appliance that comes with 12 different cooking operations like Air frying, baking, roasting, toasting, dehydrating, preheating, keep warm, pizza, slow cooking, broiling, defrosting, and fermentation. The font large glass will help to see the cooking process. The oven comes with a big digital display panel with touch control buttons. The Cosori oven works on a hot air circulation technique in which hot air is circulated around the food with the help of a convection fan. It makes your food crisp from the outside and tender from the inside.

The Cosori smart oven also connects with the smart device through Wi-Fi connectivity. It gives you remote access to your appliances. You can operate all the functions through the VeSync app except start the cooking process due to security reasons. The app also supports voice commands through Alexa and Google Assistant. The oven comes with a large cooking capacity, so it is capable to hold 12-inch pizza, whole chicken, 4 slices of bread for toasting, and more.

This cookbook contains healthy and delicious recipes comes from different categories like breakfast, beef, lamb, pork, poultry, seafood, fish, dehydrate, vegetables, side dishes, desserts, appetizer, and snacks. The recipes written in this book are unique and written into an easily understandable form. All the recipes start with their preparation and cooking time followed by step-by-step cooking instructions. At the end of each recipe, nutritional value information is written. The nutritional value information will help to keep track of daily calorie intake. The book also includes 30 days meal plan. There are few books available in the market on this topic thanks for choosing my cookbook. I hope you love and enjoy all the recipes written in this book.

Chapter 1: The Basics of COSORI Smart Air Fryer Toaster Oven

What is COSORI Smart Air Fryer Toaster Oven?

The Cosori smart air fryer toaster oven is one of the most popular advanced and multifunctional smart cooking devices. Smart functions make it unique and smart kitchen gadgets. You can easily control your Cosori smart air fryer oven remotely turn ON and OFF oven fan and oven light, also get a notification on your device by using Alexa, VeSync App, or Google Assistant. The oven is made from steel metal and comes with a powder coating over it. The interior of the oven is made up of non-stick BPA-free and PFOA-free coating. It requires 1800 Watts power to cook your food faster and having 6 heating elements to generate a maximum 450°F temperature to cook your food faster and evenly. The oven is also equipped with a super convection fan which circulates hot air around the food to get faster and crisper cooking results every time.

The Cosori smart air fryer oven is one of the 12 in 1 versatile cooking devices loaded with 12 different cooking functions like Preheat, keep warm, Air fry, Dehydrate, Bake, Pizza, Toast, Slow cook, Toast, Defrost, Broil, and Ferment. The oven comes with a big digital display panel and easy to use touch button system. Its 26 qt large cooking capacity allows holding a 12-inch pizza, 4 slices of bread, whole chicken, and more at a single cooking cycle. The Cosori air fryer oven is one of the healthy cooking appliances that cook your meal by using 85% fewer fats and oils compare with the traditional deep-frying method. If you are following any diet or want a low-calorie healthy meal, then Cosori smart air fryer oven is one of the best options available in the market.

COSORI Control Panel System

The Cosori smart air fryer toaster oven comes with a touch button control panel system. It is easy to operate the following control panel buttons and their information will help you to operate your Cosori smart oven.

- **Control Knob**

The control knob is used to navigate and select the desire cooking functions given by the display panel. Turn the knob to select the functions which blink on the digital display.

After pressing the TEMP/TIME button you can turn the knob to set the desired time and temperature settings. The clockwise turn will increase the TEMP/TIME settings and turn the knob counter clockwise to decrease the settings.

After selecting the desire settings or functions press the control knob to confirm the selection. If you press the control knob twice it again allows you to change the settings or functions.

To reset the default settings or to save the new settings press and hold the control knob for few seconds.

- **Power Button**

The power button is used to ON and OFF the oven.

To cancel the current cooking process, press the power button the oven goes standby mode.

If you press and hold the power button for 5 seconds it will pair your oven to your VeSync app.

If you want to reset your oven at factory settings the press and hold the power button for 15 seconds to reset all function settings.

- **TEMP/TIME Button**

This setting is used to adjust the temperature and time settings.

Once press the button allows you to change the temperature settings and twice press allows you to change the time settings.

After pressing the TEMP/TIME button turn the control knob clockwise and counter clockwise to increase and decrease settings respectively.

If you want to switch between Fahrenheit to Celsius then press and hold the button for few seconds.

- **START/PAUSE Button**

Using this button, you can Start and Pause cooking functions.

After finishing preheating the button blinks. Then press again to start the cooking process.

To change the cooking function during the cooking process using this button.

- **SHAKE Button**

To add or remove shake reminder use this button.

The shake reminder appears on the screen at half of the cooking time, and it will continue to blink after every 60 seconds until to open the oven door and shake food.

You can't use this function during preheating and toasting.

Press and hold the Shake button for 5 seconds to reset all functions to its factory settings.

- **Fan/Light Button**

Press this button to ON/OFF the convection fan.

When you are using air fry or dehydrate functions the fan automatically on and off. You can use a fan with all cooking functions.

Press and hold the fan/light button to turn ON/OFF the interior light of the oven.

- **Preheat Button**

Use this function to preheat the oven.

After selecting the cooking function press preheat button to add preheating before starting the actual cooking process.

COSORI Smart Function

To access the Cosori Smart function you need the VeSync app. These smart functions include:

- **Remote Control**

To control all functions remotely by using this function except stating cooking (due to safety reasons).

You can monitor the entire cooking process remotely.

- **Cosori Recipes (In-App)**

Some preprogramed recipes are available in the app. When you select these recipes you never need to set a time to send temperature settings.

You can also create and save your custom recipes.

- **Third-Party Voice Control**

You can also give voice commands through Google and Alexa assistant to operate the functions.

How to Use Cosori Smart Air Fryer Toaster Oven?

Before First Use

- First remove all packaging materials, tapes, stickers, etc. from the inside and outside surface of the oven.
- Place oven at flat and heat resistant surface.
- Remove all the accessories from the oven for cleaning. After finishing the cleaning process dry and fix the accessories into the oven.

Actual Cooking Method

- Plug the power cable into a power socket and switch it on.
- First, select the desire cooking function by rotating the control knob then press preheat button to activate preheating for that function.
- When the oven is preheated then it gives a beep. Now open the oven door and start the cooking process by pressing the start button.
- While using the preset program you never need to worry about temperature and time settings. You can also change the setting by pressing the TEMP/TIME button and rotate the control knob to adjust settings.
- If you are set SHAKE reminder then it will blink halfway through the cooking time. It will continue blinking after every 60 seconds until you have opened the oven door for shaking.
- After finishing the countdown timer oven beeps. It indicates that the cooking process is finished, and your food is ready to serve.

Benefits of Cosori Smart Air Fryer Toaster Oven

1. Multi-Purpose Cooking

The Cosori smart air fryer oven is one of the multipurpose cooking appliances that come with 12 in 1 cooking functions. These functions include Air Fry, Preheating, Broiling, Roasting, Toasting, Pizza, Keep Warm, Slow Cooking, Dehydrating, Fermentation, Defrost, and baking. A single cooking appliance provides a variety of different cooking functions into single appliances. You never need to buy separate appliances for each cooking function.

2. Healthy Cooking Appliance

The Cosori smart air fryer oven cooks your food into very little oil and fats. It cooks your healthy food by using 85% fewer fats and oils compare with the traditional deep-frying method. Fewer fats mean less calorie intake. If you are following any diet or want to lose your extra weight, then the Cosori air fryer toaster oven is one of the best choices for you. It also air fry your favourite food without compromising the taste and texture like deep-fried food.

3. Fast and Even Cooking Results

The oven works on 1800W power and having 6 heating elements to produce a maximum 450°F temperature. The super convection fan helps to circulate hot air into the cooking area. The hot air circulation will help you to make your food crisp and you will get more even and faster-cooking results every time you cook your favorite food.

4. Smart Control System

The Cosori air fryer oven is equipped with smart Wi-Fi connectivity so you can operate your oven remotely with the help of the sync app. Using this app you can adjust the time and temperature, monitor the current cooking process, browse recipes, connect to voice command controls like Alexa, Google assistant and do all the tasks remotely except Start the cooking process due to security reasons.

5. Safe to use

The Cosori air fryer toaster oven is loaded with safety features like auto-shutoff due to overheating or do not operate. When the cooking process is complete the oven will automatically shut down. While cooking oven is closed from all sides so there is no risk of splatter and accidental burns while cooking your food.

6. Easy to clean

The inner cooking area of the Cosori oven is made from BPA-free nonstick coatings. The accessories like wire rack, food tray, and fry basket are dishwasher safe. So you can easily clean it into a dishwasher.

Care and Maintenance

This is one of the essential cleaning processes done with each use of the Cosori smart air fryer oven. The following step-by-step cleaning instructions will help to clean your oven.

1. Before starting the actual cleaning process first unplug the oven and let it cool down at room temperature.
2. Open the oven door and remove the accessories like fry basket, food tray, wire rack

for cleaning. The accessories are dishwasher safe clean it into the dishwasher or use warm soapy water, sponge, and damp cloth to clean the accessories.

3. Clean the interior of the oven with the help of a soft plastic scouring pad, damp sponge. Wipe interior with a soft damp cloth.

4. Clean the outer body of the oven with the help of a soft damp cloth.

5. After finishing the cleaning process make sure all the parts are dry thoroughly. Then fix the accessories and parts with their original position.

6. Now your oven is ready for next use.

Chapter 2: Breakfast

Sausage Casserole Omelet

Preparation Time: 10 minutes
Cooking Time: 25 minutes
Serve: 12

Ingredients:

- 7 eggs
- 1 tsp mustard
- 2 cups cheddar cheese, shredded
- 3/4 cup heavy whipping cream
- 1/4 onion, chopped
- 1/2 bell pepper, chopped
- 1 lb breakfast sausage
- 1/4 tsp pepper
- 1/2 tsp salt

Directions:

1. Preheat the cosori air fryer toaster oven to 350 F.
2. Grease 9*13-inch casserole dish and set aside.
3. Brown sausage in a pan over medium-high heat. Add onion and bell pepper and sauté until onion is softened.
4. In a bowl, mix together eggs, mustard, 1 1/2 cups cheese, heavy cream, pepper, and salt. Add sausage, onion, and bell pepper, and mix well.
5. Pour egg mixture into the prepared casserole dish.
6. Place casserole dish on the wire rack, then place the rack at mid-position in the toaster oven.
7. Select the bake mode and set the time to 20 minutes. Press starts.
8. Serve and enjoy.

Nutritional Value (Amount per Serving):

- Calories 271
- Fat 22.4 g
- Carbohydrates 1.4 g
- Sugar 0.7 g
- Protein 15.6 g
- Cholesterol 157 mg

Healthy Baked Oatmeal

Preparation Time: 10 minutes

Cooking Time: 40 minutes

Serve: 9

Ingredients:

- 2 eggs
- 1/2 cup applesauce
- 1/4 cup coconut oil, melted
- 1 cup milk
- 1 1/2 tsp vanilla
- 1 tsp cinnamon
- 2 tsp baking powder
- 1/2 cup brown sugar
- 3 cups old-fashioned oats
- 1/2 tsp salt

Directions:

1. Preheat the cosori air fryer toaster oven to 350 F.
2. Grease 9*9-inch baking dish and set aside.
3. In a bowl, mix oats, baking powder, sugar, cinnamon, and salt. Set aside.
4. In a separate bowl, whisk eggs with milk, applesauce, oil, and vanilla.
5. Add oats mixture into the egg mixture and mix until well combined.
6. Pour mixture into the prepared baking dish.
7. Place baking dish on the wire rack, then place the rack at mid-position in the toaster oven.
8. Select the bake mode and set the time to 40 minutes. Press start.
9. Slice and enjoy.

Nutritional Value (Amount per Serving):

- Calories 220
- Fat 9.6 g
- Carbohydrates 29.7 g
- Sugar 11.3 g
- Protein 5.5 g
- Cholesterol 39 mg

Sausage Hashbrown Casserole

Preparation Time: 10 minutes

Cooking Time: 35 minutes

Serve: 8

Ingredients:

- 10 eggs
- 1 cup cheddar cheese, shredded
- 1/2 cup milk
- 1 1/2 cup spinach, chopped
- 2 cups frozen hashbrowns
- 3/4 cup onion, chopped
- 3/4 cup bell pepper, chopped
- 1 lb breakfast sausage
- 1/2 tsp pepper
- 1 tsp salt

Directions:

1. Preheat the cosori air fryer toaster oven to 350 F.
2. Grease 9*13-inch baking dish and set aside.
3. Add sausage, bell pepper, and onion in a pan and cook over medium-high heat until onion is softened.
4. Add spinach and cook for 1-2 minutes. Remove pan from heat and let it cool.
5. In a bowl, add the remaining ingredients and mix well. Add sausage mixture and mix until well combined.
6. Pour mixture into the prepared baking dish.
7. Place baking dish on the wire rack, then place the rack at mid-position in the toaster oven.
8. Select the bake mode and set the time to 30 minutes. Press starts.
9. Slice and enjoy.

Nutritional Value (Amount per Serving):

- Calories 377
- Fat 28.6 g
- Carbohydrates 7.7 g
- Sugar 2.2 g
- Protein 22.6 g
- Cholesterol 268 mg

Easy Cheesy Breakfast Casserole

Preparation Time: 10 minutes
Cooking Time: 40 minutes
Serve: 8

Ingredients:

- 8 eggs
- 28 oz hashbrown potatoes, thawed
- 2 cups almond milk
- 1 1/2 cups cheddar cheese, shredded
- 1 lb bacon, cooked & crumbled
- Pepper
- Salt

Directions:

1. Preheat the cosori air fryer toaster oven to 350 F.
2. Grease 9*13-inch baking dish and set aside.
3. In a bowl, mix hashbrowns, 1 cup cheese, bacon, and salt and pour into the prepared baking dish.
4. In a separate bowl, whisk eggs with pepper and milk.
5. Pour egg mixture over hashbrown mixture and sprinkle with remaining cheese.
6. Place baking dish on the wire rack, then place the rack at mid-position in the toaster oven.
7. Select the bake mode and set the time to 40 minutes. Press start.
8. Slice and enjoy.

Nutritional Value (Amount per Serving):

- Calories 649
- Fat 49.4 g
- Carbohydrates 18.2 g
- Sugar 3.5 g
- Protein 34.3 g
- Cholesterol 248 mg

Ham Bacon Breakfast Casserole

Preparation Time: 10 minutes
Cooking Time: 35 minutes
Serve: 12

Ingredients:

- 12 eggs
- 4 oz can green chilies, chopped
- 1/2 onion, chopped
- 2 cups cheddar cheese, grated
- 5 bacon slices, cooked & crumbled
- 1 lb ham, cubed
- 1/2 cup milk
- 1/2 tsp pepper
- 1/2 tsp salt

Directions:

1. Preheat the cosori air fryer toaster oven to 350 F.
2. Grease 9*13-inch baking dish and set aside.
3. In a bowl, whisk eggs with milk until well combined.
4. Add onion, green chilies, cheese, bacon, ham, pepper, and salt, and stir well to combine.
5. Pour mixture into the prepared baking dish.
6. Place baking dish on the wire rack, then place the rack at mid-position in the toaster oven.
7. Select the bake mode and set the time to 35 minutes. Press starts.
8. Slice and enjoy.

Nutritional Value (Amount per Serving):

- Calories 252
- Fat 17.4 g
- Carbohydrates 3.6 g
- Sugar 1.1 g
- Protein 19.9 g
- Cholesterol 215 mg

Healthy Baked Frittata

Preparation Time: 10 minutes
Cooking Time: 45 minutes
Serve: 10

Ingredients:

- 10 eggs
- 10 oz cheddar cheese, grated
- 1 tsp Dijon mustard
- 3/4 cup milk
- 1/2 cup cream
- 5 bacon, cooked & chopped
- 1 lb sausage
- 1/4 tsp pepper
- 1/2 tsp sea salt

Directions:

1. Preheat the cosori air fryer toaster oven to 350 F.
2. Grease 13*9-inch baking dish and set aside.
3. Add sausage to a pan and cook over medium heat until sausage is no longer pink.
4. In a bowl, whisk eggs with milk, cream, mustard, pepper, and salt.
5. Add cheese into the prepared baking dish and top with sausage and bacon.
6. Pour egg mixture over sausage mixture.
7. Place baking dish on the wire rack, then place the rack at mid-position in the toaster oven.
8. Select the bake mode and set the time to 45 minutes. Press start.
9. Slice and enjoy.

Nutritional Value (Amount per Serving):

- Calories 400
- Fat 31.7 g
- Carbohydrates 2.2 g
- Sugar 1.6 g
- Protein 25.7 g
- Cholesterol 246 mg

Zucchini Egg Bake

Preparation Time: 10 minutes

Cooking Time: 45 minutes

Serve: 6

Ingredients:

- 3 eggs
- 1/2 cup flour
- 1/2 cup cheddar cheese, grated
- 1/2 cup feta cheese, crumbled
- 3 zucchinis, grated
- Pepper
- Salt

Directions:

1. Preheat the cosori air fryer toaster oven to 350 F.
2. Grease a 9-inch baking dish and set it aside.
3. In a bowl, mix zucchini, cheeses, eggs, pepper, and salt. Slowly add flour and mix well.
4. Pour mixture into the prepared baking dish.
5. Place baking dish on the wire rack, then place the rack at mid-position in the toaster oven.
6. Select the bake mode and set the time to 45 minutes. Press starts.
7. Slice and enjoy.

Nutritional Value (Amount per Serving):

- Calories 156
- Fat 8.3 g
- Carbohydrates 12 g
- Sugar 2.5 g
- Protein 9.2 g
- Cholesterol 103 mg

Spicy Egg Muffins

Preparation Time: 10 minutes
Cooking Time: 15 minutes
Serve: 12

Ingredients:

- 10 eggs
- 1/3 cup bacon, cooked & chopped
- 1/2 cup cheddar cheese, grated
- 1/3 cup cream cheese, softened
- 4 jalapeno peppers, chopped
- 1/2 tsp garlic powder
- Pepper
- Salt

Directions:

1. Preheat the cosori air fryer toaster oven to 400 F.
2. Spray muffin pan with cooking spray and set aside.
3. In a bowl, whisk eggs with garlic powder, pepper, and salt.
4. Add remaining ingredients and stir well to combine.
5. Pour batter into the prepared muffin pan.
6. Place muffin pan on the wire rack, then place the rack at mid-position in the toaster oven.
7. Select the bake mode and set the time to 15 minutes. Press starts.
8. Serve and enjoy.

Nutritional Value (Amount per Serving):

- Calories 99
- Fat 7.7 g
- Carbohydrates 1 g
- Sugar 0.5 g
- Protein 6.6 g
- Cholesterol 149 mg

Pumpkin Pie Oatmeal

Preparation Time: 10 minutes
Cooking Time: 40 minutes
Serve: 6

Ingredients:

- 2 eggs
- 1 tsp vanilla
- 2 tbsp butter, melted
- 2 cups milk
- 1 cup pumpkin puree
- 2 tsp pumpkin pie spice
- 2 tsp baking powder
- 1/4 cup brown sugar
- 1/4 cup sugar
- 3 cups old-fashioned oats
- 1/4 tsp salt

Directions:

1. Preheat the cosori air fryer toaster oven to 350 F.
2. Spray 8*8-inch baking dish with cooking spray and set aside.
3. In a bowl, mix oats, pumpkin pie spice, baking powder, brown sugar, sugar, and salt and set aside.
4. In a separate bowl, whisk eggs, vanilla, butter, milk, and pumpkin puree until smooth.
5. Add oat mixture into the egg mixture and stir well to combine.
6. Pour mixture into the prepared baking dish.
7. Place baking dish on the wire rack, then place the rack at mid-position in the toaster oven.
8. Select the bake mode and set the time to 40 minutes. Press start.
9. Serve and enjoy.

Nutritional Value (Amount per Serving):

- Calories 319
- Fat 10.2 g
- Carbohydrates 49.9 g
- Sugar 20.5 g
- Protein 10.1 g
- Cholesterol 71 mg

Mushroom Asparagus Egg Bake

Preparation Time: 10 minutes
Cooking Time: 50 minutes
Serve: 8

Ingredients:

- 10 eggs
- 1/2 cup milk
- 2 cups cheddar cheese, shredded
- 2 cups mushrooms, sliced
- 2 cups asparagus, diced
- 2 tbsp onion, minced
- 2 tbsp butter
- 1/4 tsp pepper
- 1/2 tsp kosher salt

Directions:

1. Preheat the cosori air fryer toaster oven to 350 F.
2. Grease 2-quart casserole dish and set aside.
3. Melt butter in a pan over medium heat. Add onion and sauté for a minute.
4. Add mushrooms and asparagus and sauté for 5 minutes.
5. Transfer sautéed vegetables into the prepared casserole dish and top with cheese.
6. In a separate bowl, whisk eggs with milk, pepper, and salt and pour over cheese.
7. Place casserole dish on the wire rack, then place the rack at mid-position in the toaster oven.
8. Select the bake mode and set the time to 40 minutes. Press starts.
9. Serve and enjoy.

Nutritional Value (Amount per Serving):

- Calories 211
- Fat 16.1 g
- Carbohydrates 3.3 g
- Sugar 2 g
- Protein 14.1 g
- Cholesterol 216 mg

Broccoli Egg Bake

Preparation Time: 10 minutes
Cooking Time: 45 minutes
Serve: 6

Ingredients:

- 10 eggs
- 1/4 tsp garlic powder
- 3 cups broccoli florets
- 1 cup cottage cheese
- 1/2 tsp pepper
- 1/2 tsp salt

Directions:

1. Preheat the cosori air fryer toaster oven to 375 F.
2. Grease 8*8-inch baking dish and set aside.
3. In a bowl, whisk eggs with pepper and salt.
4. Add remaining ingredients and stir well to combine.
5. Pour egg mixture into the prepared baking dish.
6. Place baking dish on the wire rack, then place the rack at mid-position in the toaster oven.
7. Select the bake mode and set the time to 45 minutes. Press starts.
8. Serve and enjoy.

Nutritional Value (Amount per Serving):

- Calories 155
- Fat 8.2 g
- Carbohydrates 5.2 g
- Sugar 1.5 g
- Protein 15.7 g
- Cholesterol 276 mg

Cheddar Kale Egg Cups

Preparation Time: 10 minutes

Cooking Time: 15 minutes

Serve: 6

Ingredients:

- 5 eggs
- 3 oz cheddar cheese, shredded
- 1 cup kale, chopped
- 1/4 tsp garlic powder
- Pepper
- Salt

Directions:

1. Preheat the cosori air fryer toaster oven to 400 F.
2. Spray muffin pan with cooking spray and set aside.
3. In a bowl, whisk eggs with garlic powder, pepper, and salt.
4. Add cheese and kale and stir well.
5. Pour egg mixture into the muffin pan.
6. Place muffin pan on the wire rack, then place the rack at mid-position in the toaster oven.
7. Select the bake mode and set the time to 15 minutes. Press starts.
8. Serve and enjoy.

Nutritional Value (Amount per Serving):

- Calories 116
- Fat 8.3 g
- Carbohydrates 1.7 g
- Sugar 0.4 g
- Protein 8.5 g
- Cholesterol 151 mg

Artichoke Spinach Bake

Preparation Time: 10 minutes
Cooking Time: 35 minutes
Serve: 8

Ingredients:

- 8 eggs
- 1/2 cup feta cheese, crumbled
- 2 tbsp parmesan cheese, grated
- 1/4 cup milk
- 4 egg whites
- 1/3 cup bell pepper, diced
- 3/4 cup artichoke, chopped
- 1/2 cup green onions, chopped
- 10 oz frozen spinach, thawed & chopped
- Pepper
- Salt

Directions:

1. Preheat the cosori air fryer toaster oven to 375 F.
2. Spray 9*13-inch casserole dish with cooking spray and set aside.
3. In a bowl, mix spinach, bell pepper, green onion, and artichoke and pour into the prepared casserole dish.
4. In a separate bowl, whisk eggs, milk, egg whites, parmesan cheese, pepper, and salt. Add feta cheese and mix well.
5. Pour egg mixture over vegetables.
6. Place casserole dish on the wire rack, then place the rack at mid-position in the toaster oven.
7. Select the bake mode and set the time to 35 minutes. Press starts.
8. Serve and enjoy.

Nutritional Value (Amount per Serving):

- Calories 140
- Fat 8.2 g
- Carbohydrates 4.9 g
- Sugar 1.9 g
- Protein 12.7 g
- Cholesterol 178 mg

Hashbrown Mushroom Casserole

Preparation Time: 10 minutes

Cooking Time: 35 minutes

Serve: 12

Ingredients:

- 4 eggs
- 2 tbsp rosemary, chopped
- 6 oz cheddar cheese, shredded
- 10.5 oz cream of mushroom soup
- 8 oz sour cream
- 35 oz shredded potatoes
- 1 tbsp butter
- 1 tbsp garlic, minced
- 1/2 small onion, chopped
- 4 oz mushrooms, chopped
- Pepper
- Salt

Directions:

1. Preheat the cosori air fryer toaster oven to 375 F.
2. Spray 9*13-inch baking dish with cooking spray and set aside.
3. Melt butter in a pan over medium heat. Add garlic, onions, and mushrooms and sauté until onion is softened. Season with pepper and salt.
4. In a bowl, mix shredded potatoes, cheese, soup, sour cream, eggs, rosemary, and sautéed onion and mushrooms.
5. Pour mixture into the prepared baking dish.
6. Place baking dish on the wire rack, then place the rack at mid-position in the toaster oven.
7. Select the bake mode and set the time to 30 minutes. Press starts.
8. Serve and enjoy.

Nutritional Value (Amount per Serving):

- Calories 201
- Fat 12 g
- Carbohydrates 16.7 g
- Sugar 1.6 g
- Protein 8 g
- Cholesterol 80 mg

Broccoli Egg Bake

Preparation Time: 10 minutes
Cooking Time: 30 minutes
Serve: 4

Ingredients:

- 12 eggs
- 2 cups broccoli florets
- 1 cup grape tomatoes, halved
- 1/2 cup cheddar cheese, shredded
- 1/2 onion, chopped
- 1/4 tsp garlic powder
- Pepper
- Salt

Directions:

1. Preheat the cosori air fryer toaster oven to 325 F.
2. Spray a baking dish with cooking spray and set it aside.
3. Add broccoli florets and tomatoes into the baking dish and mix well.
4. In a bowl, whisk eggs with cheese, onion, garlic powder, pepper, and salt.
5. Pour egg mixture over broccoli and tomatoes.
6. Place baking dish on the wire rack, then place the rack at mid-position in the toaster oven.
7. Select the bake mode and set the time to 30 minutes. Press starts.
8. Serve and enjoy.

Nutritional Value (Amount per Serving):

- Calories 275
- Fat 18.1 g
- Carbohydrates 7.4 g
- Sugar 3.7 g
- Protein 22 g
- Cholesterol 506 mg

Chapter 3: Poultry Recipes

Delicious Chicken with Mushrooms

Preparation Time: 10 minutes

Cooking Time: 30 minutes

Serve: 4

Ingredients:

- 2 lbs chicken breasts, halved
- 1/3 cup sun-dried tomatoes
- 8 oz mushrooms, sliced
- 1/2 cup mayonnaise
- 1 tsp salt

Directions:

1. Preheat the cosori air fryer toaster oven to 400 F.
2. Place chicken breasts into the greased baking dish and top with sun-dried tomatoes, mushrooms, mayonnaise, and salt. Mix well.
3. Place baking dish on the wire rack, then place the rack at mid-position in the toaster oven.
4. Select the bake mode and set the time to 30 minutes. Press starts.
5. Serve and enjoy.

Nutritional Value (Amount per Serving):

- Calories 568
- Fat 41.5 g
- Carbohydrates 3.2 g
- Sugar 2 g
- Protein 68 g
- Cholesterol 202 mg

Tasty Chicken Casserole

Preparation Time: 10 minutes
Cooking Time: 40 minutes
Serve: 8

Ingredients:

- 2 lbs cooked chicken, shredded
- 5 oz Swiss cheese
- 1 oz fresh lemon juice
- 1 tbsp Dijon mustard
- 6 oz cream cheese, softened
- 4 oz butter, melted
- 6 oz ham, cut into small pieces
- 1/2 tsp salt

Directions:

1. Preheat the cosori air fryer toaster oven to 350 F.
2. Place chicken into the baking dish then top with ham.
3. Add butter, lemon juice, mustard, cream cheese, and salt into the blender and blend until smooth.
4. Spread butter mixture over chicken and ham mixture. Arrange Swiss cheese slices on top.
5. Place baking dish on the wire rack, then place the rack at mid-position in the toaster oven.
6. Select the bake mode and set the time to 40 minutes. Press starts.
7. Serve and enjoy.

Nutritional Value (Amount per Serving):

- Calories 451
- Fat 29.2 g
- Carbohydrates 2.5 g
- Sugar 0.4 g
- Protein 43 g
- Cholesterol 170 mg

Flavorful Chicken Stew

Preparation Time: 10 minutes

Cooking Time: 4 hours

Serve: 8

Ingredients:

- 3 lbs chicken thighs, skinless and boneless
- 2 cups onion, chopped
- 1 tsp dried thyme
- 2 bay leaves
- 2 tsp Cajun seasoning
- 1 cup chicken broth, low sodium
- 15 oz tomatoes, chopped
- 2 tbsp olive oil
- 6 oz tomato paste
- 6 garlic cloves, chopped
- 2 cups green bell pepper, chopped
- 2 cups celery, chopped
- 1/4 tsp pepper

Directions:

1. Heat olive oil in a pan over medium heat.
2. Add garlic, onion, bell pepper, and celery and sauté for 5-7 minutes.
3. Add tomato paste and sauté for 2 minutes.
4. Transfer pan mixture into the pot.
5. Add tomatoes, thyme, bay leaves, Cajun seasoning, chicken broth, and black pepper into the pot and stir well.
6. Add chicken and stir well. Cover pot with foil.
7. Place pot on the wire rack then places the rack at a low position in the toaster oven.
8. Select the slow cook mode and set the time to 4 hours. Press start.
9. Stir well and serve.

Nutritional Value (Amount per Serving):

- Calories 400
- Fat 16.6 g
- Carbohydrates 4.9 g
- Sugar 4.9 g
- Protein 51.4 g
- Cholesterol 151 mg

Lemon Chicken

Preparation Time: 10 minutes
Cooking Time: 35 minutes
Serve: 4

Ingredients:

- 4 chicken breasts, skinless and boneless, cut into chunks
- 2 tsp garlic, minced
- 2 tbsp lemon juice
- 2 tbsp smoked paprika
- 3 tbsp olive oil
- Pepper
- Salt

Directions:

1. Preheat the cosori air fryer toaster oven to 350 F.
2. In a small bowl, mix garlic, lemon juice, paprika, and olive oil. Season chicken with pepper and salt.
3. Spread 1/3 bowl mixture on the bottom of the casserole dish.
4. Add seasoned chicken into the casserole dish and rub with fish sauce.
5. Pour remaining sauce over chicken and rub well.
6. Place baking dish on the wire rack, then place the rack at mid-position in the toaster oven.
7. Select the bake mode and set the time to 35 minutes. Press starts.
8. Serve and enjoy.

Nutritional Value (Amount per Serving):

- Calories 381
- Fat 21.8 g
- Carbohydrates 2.6 g
- Sugar 0.5 g
- Protein 42.9 g
- Cholesterol 130 mg

Pepper Artichoke Chicken

Preparation Time: 10 minutes
Cooking Time: 2 hours
Serve: 6

Ingredients:

- 2 1/2 lbs chicken thighs, skinless and boneless
- 1/2 cup olives
- 2 tsp dried garlic, minced
- 2 tbsp olive oil
- 1 cup roasted peppers, drained and cut into chunks
- 1 tsp dried oregano
- 14 oz can artichokes
- 3 tbsp lemon juice
- 1/2 tsp pepper
- 1 tsp salt

Directions:

1. Add chicken to the pot.
2. Add remaining ingredients on top of the chicken and stir well to combine. Cover pot with foil.
3. Place pot on the wire rack then places the rack at a low position in the toaster oven.
4. Select the slow cook mode and set the time to 2 hours. Press starts.
5. Stir well and serve.

Nutritional Value (Amount per Serving):

- Calories 424
- Fat 20 g
- Carbohydrates 3.3 g
- Sugar 1.5 g
- Protein 55.2 g
- Cholesterol 168 mg

Baked Chicken Skewers

Preparation Time: 10 minutes
Cooking Time: 20 minutes
Serve: 4

Ingredients:

- 1 1/2 lbs chicken breast, cut into 1-inch cubes
- For marinade:
- 1 tbsp red wine vinegar
- 1/2 cup yogurt
- 2 tbsp fresh rosemary, chopped
- 1/4 tsp cayenne
- 2 tbsp dried oregano
- 1/4 cup fresh mint leaves
- 5 garlic cloves
- 1/2 cup lemon juice
- 1 cup olive oil
- Pepper
- Salt

Directions:

1. Preheat the cosori air fryer toaster oven to 400 F.
2. Add all marinade ingredients into the blender and blend until smooth.
3. Pour marinade in a bowl.
4. Add chicken to the bowl and coat well. Cover and place in the refrigerator for 1 hour.
5. Thread marinated chicken onto the skewers.
6. Place skewers onto the baking sheet.
7. Place baking sheet on the wire rack, then place the rack at mid-position in the toaster oven.
8. Select the bake mode and set the time to 20 minutes. Press starts.
9. Serve and enjoy.

Nutritional Value (Amount per Serving):

- Calories 677
- Fat 55.8 g
- Carbohydrates 7.1 g
- Sugar 3 g
- Protein 38.8 g
- Cholesterol 111 mg

Meatballs

Preparation Time: 10 minutes

Cooking Time: 25 minutes

Serve: 6

Ingredients:

- 1 egg, lightly beaten
- 1 lb ground turkey
- 2 tbsp almond flour
- 1/2 tsp ground ginger
- 1 tsp olive oil
- 2 tbsp chives, chopped
- 1/2 tsp salt

Directions:

1. Preheat the cosori air fryer toaster oven to 375 F.
2. In a bowl, combine together turkey, chives, almond flour, olive oil, ginger, egg, and salt until just combined.
3. Make small balls from the meat mixture and place them onto the baking sheet.
4. Place baking sheet on the wire rack, then place the rack at mid-position in the toaster oven.
5. Select the bake mode and set the time to 25 minutes. Press starts.
6. Serve and enjoy.

Nutritional Value (Amount per Serving):

- Calories 219
- Fat 14.5 g
- Carbohydrates 2.2 g
- Sugar 0.4 g
- Protein 23.6 g
- Cholesterol 104 mg

Tasty Chili Chicken

Preparation Time: 10 minutes
Cooking Time: 6 hours
Serve: 5

Ingredients:

- 1 lb chicken breasts, skinless and boneless
- 1/2 tsp dried sage
- 1/2 tsp cumin
- 1 tsp dried oregano
- 12 oz can green chilies
- 14 oz can tomato, diced
- 2 cups of water
- 1 jalapeno pepper, chopped
- 1 poblano pepper, chopped
- 1/2 tsp paprika
- 1/2 cup dried chives
- 1 tsp sea salt

Directions:

1. Add all ingredients into the pot and stir well to combine. Cover pot with foil.
2. Place pot on the wire rack then places the rack at a low position in the toaster oven.
3. Select the slow cook mode and set the time to 6 hours. Press starts.
4. Remove chicken from pot and shred using a fork.
5. Serve and enjoy.

Nutritional Value (Amount per Serving):

- Calories 212
- Fat 7.1 g
- Carbohydrates 8.9 g
- Sugar 3.4 g
- Protein 27.9 g
- Cholesterol 81 mg

Simple Turkey Breast

Preparation Time: 10 minutes

Cooking Time: 4 hours

Serve: 12

Ingredients:

- 6 lbs turkey breast, bone-in
- 1/2 cup chicken stock
- 3 fresh rosemary sprigs
- Pepper
- Salt

Directions:

1. Season turkey breast with pepper and salt and place in the pot. Cover pot with foil.
2. Add stock and rosemary on top of turkey breast.
3. Place pot on the wire rack then places the rack at a low position in the toaster oven.
4. Select the slow cook mode and set the time to 4 hours. Press starts.
5. Serve and enjoy.

Nutritional Value (Amount per Serving):

- Calories 237
- Fat 3.8 g
- Carbohydrates 9.8 g
- Sugar 8 g
- Protein 38.7 g
- Cholesterol 98 mg

Italian Chicken

Preparation Time: 10 minutes
Cooking Time: 6 hours
Serve: 4

Ingredients:

- 4 chicken breasts, skinless and boneless
- 1 cup chicken stock
- 1/4 cup fresh lemon juice
- 2 tsp dried oregano
- 1 tbsp garlic, minced
- 3/4 tbsp lemon zest
- 1 tsp kosher salt

Directions:

1. Add all ingredients into the pot and stir well to combine. Cover pot with foil.
2. Place pot on the wire rack then places the rack at a low position in the toaster oven.
3. Select the slow cook mode and set the time to 6 hours. Press starts.
4. Stir well and serve.

Nutritional Value (Amount per Serving):

- Calories 291
- Fat 11.2 g
- Carbohydrates 2.1 g
- Sugar 0.6 g
- Protein 42.9 g
- Cholesterol 130 mg

Yummy Chicken Shawarma

Preparation Time: 10 minutes
Cooking Time: 3 hours
Serve: 5

Ingredients:

- 1 1/4 lbs chicken thigh, skinless and boneless
- 1 1/2 tbsp tahini
- 1/4 tsp ground coriander
- 1/4 tsp cinnamon
- 1/2 tsp curry powder
- 1/2 tsp dried parsley
- 1 tsp cumin
- 2 tbsp garlic, minced
- 1/2 cup Greek yogurt
- 1/4 cup chicken stock
- 1/4 cup fresh lemon juice
- 1 tsp paprika
- 1 tsp garlic powder
- 1 tbsp olive oil
- Pepper
- Salt

Directions:

1. Add all ingredients into the pot and stir well to combine. Cover pot with foil.
2. Place pot on the wire rack then places the rack at a low position in the toaster oven.
3. Select the slow cook mode and set the time to 3 hours. Press starts.
4. Stir well and serve.

Nutritional Value (Amount per Serving):

- Calories 295
- Fat 14.3 g
- Carbohydrates 4.2 g
- Sugar 1.4 g
- Protein 36.2 g
- Cholesterol 102 mg

Chicken with Artichokes & Olives

Preparation Time: 10 minutes

Cooking Time: 8 hours

Serve: 6

Ingredients:

- 6 chicken thighs, skinless and boneless
- 1 tsp dried oregano
- 14 olives, pitted
- 3 tbsp fresh lemon juice
- 10 oz frozen artichoke hearts
- 14 oz can tomato, diced
- 1/2 tsp garlic powder
- 1 tsp dried basil
- Pepper
- Salt

Directions:

1. Season chicken with pepper and salt and place in the pot.
2. Pour remaining ingredients over chicken. Cover pot with foil.
3. Place pot on the wire rack then places the rack at a low position in the toaster oven.
4. Select the slow cook mode and set the time to 8 hours. Press starts.
5. Stir well and serve.

Nutritional Value (Amount per Serving):

- Calories 309
- Fat 12.1 g
- Carbohydrates 4.8 g
- Sugar 2.5 g
- Protein 43.2 g
- Cholesterol 130 mg

Turkey Breast with Vegetables

Preparation Time: 10 minutes

Cooking Time: 45 minutes

Serve: 4

Ingredients:

- 1 lb turkey breast, cut into 1-inch cubes
- 1 tsp garlic powder
- 2 tbsp olive oil
- 1 cup mushrooms, cleaned
- 1/2 lb Brussels sprouts, cut in half
- Pepper
- Salt

Directions:

1. Preheat the cosori air fryer toaster oven to 350 F.
2. In a small bowl, mix oil, garlic powder, pepper, and salt.
3. In a baking dish, mix together turkey, mushrooms, and Brussels sprouts. Pour oil mixture over turkey.
4. Place baking dish on the wire rack, then place the rack at mid-position in the toaster oven.
5. Select the bake mode and set the time to 45 minutes. Press starts.
6. Serve and enjoy.

Nutritional Value (Amount per Serving):

- Calories 190
- Fat 8.3 g
- Carbohydrates 10.2 g
- Sugar 3.7 g
- Protein 20.5 g
- Cholesterol 10.2 mg

Chicken Zucchini Stew

Preparation Time: 10 minutes
Cooking Time: 4 hours
Serve: 6

Ingredients:

- 1 1/2 lbs chicken breasts, boneless & cut into chunks
- 1 tsp oregano, dried
- 8 oz mushrooms, sliced
- 6 oz tomato paste
- 1 tbsp garlic cloves, diced
- 1 tsp thyme, dried
- 1 cup chicken stock
- 3 cups zucchini, diced
- 1 onion, diced
- 1 tsp basil, dried
- 1 cup bell pepper, diced
- Salt

Directions:

1. Add all ingredients into the pot and stir well to combine. Cover pot with foil.
2. Place pot on the wire rack then places the rack at a low position in the toaster oven.
3. Select the slow cook mode and set the time to 4 hours. Press starts.
4. Stir well and serve.

Nutritional Value (Amount per Serving):

- Calories 256
- Fat 8.8 g
- Carbohydrates 8.1 g
- Sugar 4 g
- Protein 35.6 g
- Cholesterol 101 mg

Herb Chicken

Preparation Time: 10 minutes

Cooking Time: 10 minutes

Serve: 2

Ingredients:

- 2 chicken breasts, boneless and skinless
- 2 tsp garlic, minced
- 1 tsp dried thyme
- 1 tsp dried oregano
- 1 tsp dried basil
- Pepper
- Salt

Directions:

1. Preheat the cosori air fryer toaster oven to 400 F.
2. In a small bowl, mix garlic, thyme, oregano, basil, pepper, and salt and rub all over the chicken.
3. Place chicken into the baking dish.
4. Place baking dish on the wire rack, then place the rack at mid-position in the toaster oven.
5. Select the bake mode and set the time to 10 minutes. Press starts.
6. Serve and enjoy.

Nutritional Value (Amount per Serving):

- Calories 285
- Fat 11 g
- Carbohydrates 1.8 g
- Sugar 0.1 g
- Protein 42.6 g
- Cholesterol 130 mg

Classic Chicken

Preparation Time: 10 minutes

Cooking Time: 30 minutes

Serve: 4

Ingredients:

- 1 lb chicken breasts, skinless & boneless

For marinade:

- 1/2 tsp dill
- 1 tbsp lemon juice
- 3 tbsp olive oil
- 1 tsp onion powder
- 1/4 tsp basil
- 1/4 tsp oregano
- 3 garlic cloves, minced
- 1/4 tsp pepper
- 1/2 tsp salt

Directions:

1. Preheat the cosori air fryer toaster oven to 390 F.
2. Add all marinade ingredients into the bowl and mix well.
3. Add chicken into the marinade and coat well. Cover and place in the refrigerator overnight.
4. Arrange marinated chicken onto the baking sheet.
5. Place baking sheet on the wire rack, then place the rack at mid-position in the toaster oven.
6. Select the bake mode and set the time to 30 minutes. Press starts.
7. Serve and enjoy.

Nutritional Value (Amount per Serving):

- Calories 313
- Fat 19 g
- Carbohydrates 1.5 g
- Sugar 0.3 g
- Protein 33.1 g
- Cholesterol 101 mg

Broccoli Ranch Chicken

Preparation Time: 10 minutes
Cooking Time: 30 minutes
Serve: 4

Ingredients:

- 4 chicken breasts, skinless and boneless
- 5 bacon slices, cooked and chopped
- 2 cups broccoli florets, blanched and chopped
- 1/3 cup mozzarella cheese, shredded
- 1 cup cheddar cheese, shredded
- 1/2 cup ranch dressing

Directions:

1. Preheat the cosori air fryer toaster oven to 375 F.
2. Add chicken into the 13*9-inch casserole dish. Top with bacon and broccoli.
3. Pour ranch dressing over chicken and top with mozzarella cheese and cheddar cheese.
4. Place casserole dish on the wire rack, then place the rack at mid-position in the toaster oven.
5. Select the bake mode and set the time to 30 minutes. Press starts.
6. Serve and enjoy.

Nutritional Value (Amount per Serving):

- Calories 551
- Fat 30.8 g
- Carbohydrates 5.4 g
- Sugar 1.7 g
- Protein 60.4 g
- Cholesterol 187 mg

Creamy Chicken Breast

Preparation Time: 10 minutes
Cooking Time: 45 minutes
Serve: 4

Ingredients:

- 4 chicken breasts, skinless, boneless & cut into chunks
- 1 cup parmesan cheese, shredded
- 1 cup mayonnaise
- 1 tsp garlic powder
- Pepper
- Salt

Directions:

1. Preheat the cosori air fryer toaster oven to 375 F.
2. Add chicken pieces into the bowl of buttermilk and soak overnight.
3. Add marinated chicken pieces into the 9*13-inch baking dish.
4. Mix together mayonnaise, garlic powder, 1/2 cup parmesan cheese, pepper, and salt, and pour over chicken.
5. Sprinkle remaining cheese on top of the chicken.
6. Place baking dish on the wire rack, then place the rack at mid-position in the toaster oven.
7. Select the bake mode and set the time to 45 minutes. Press starts.
8. Serve and enjoy.

Nutritional Value (Amount per Serving):

- Calories 581
- Fat 35.3 g
- Carbohydrates 15.4 g
- Sugar 3.9 g
- Protein 50.1 g
- Cholesterol 161 mg

Easy Chicken Thighs

Preparation Time: 10 minutes
Cooking Time: 35 minutes
Serve: 6

Ingredients:

- 6 chicken thighs
- 2 tbsp olive oil
- 2 tsp poultry seasoning
- Pepper
- Salt

Directions:

1. Preheat the cosori air fryer toaster oven to 390 F.
2. Brush chicken with oil and rub with poultry seasoning, pepper, and salt.
3. Arrange chicken on a baking sheet.
4. Place baking sheet on the wire rack, then place the rack at mid-position in the toaster oven.
5. Select the bake mode and set the time to 35 minutes. Press starts.
6. Serve and enjoy.

Nutritional Value (Amount per Serving):

- Calories 319
- Fat 15.5 g
- Carbohydrates 0.3 g
- Sugar 0 g
- Protein 42.3 g
- Cholesterol 130 mg

Curried Chicken

Preparation Time: 10 minutes
Cooking Time: 40 minutes
Serve: 4

Ingredients:

- 4 chicken breasts, skinless and boneless
- 1/3 cup butter
- 1/3 cup honey
- 4 tsp curry powder
- 1/4 cup mustard

Directions:

1. Preheat the cosori air fryer toaster oven to 375 F.
2. Add butter and honey in a small saucepan and heat over low heat until butter is melted.
3. Remove saucepan from heat and stir in curry powder and mustard.
4. Arrange chicken in a casserole dish and pour butter mixture over chicken.
5. Place casserole dish on the wire rack, then place the rack at mid-position in the toaster oven.
6. Select the bake mode and set the time to 40 minutes. Press starts.
7. Serve and enjoy.

Nutritional Value (Amount per Serving):

- Calories 552
- Fat 29.3 g
- Carbohydrates 27.9 g
- Sugar 23.9 g
- Protein 45.2 g
- Cholesterol 171 mg

Chapter 4: Beef, Pork & Lamb

Flavorful Beef Chili

Preparation Time: 10 minutes

Cooking Time: 6 hours

Serve: 6

Ingredients:

- 1 lb ground beef
- 1 tbsp soy sauce
- 1 tbsp parsley, chopped
- 1 tsp onion powder
- 4 carrots, chopped
- 1 onion, chopped
- 1 tsp garlic powder
- 1 tsp paprika
- 2 1/2 tsp chili powder
- 1 bell pepper, seeded and chopped
- 1/2 tsp salt

Directions:

1. Add meat to the pan and cook over medium-high heat until meat is brown.
2. Transfer meat into the pot.
3. Add remaining ingredients into the pot. Cover pot with foil.
4. Place pot on the wire rack then places the rack at a low position in the toaster oven.
5. Select the slow cook mode and set the time to 6 hours. Press starts.
6. Stir well and serve.

Nutritional Value (Amount per Serving):

- Calories 207
- Fat 9.2 g
- Carbohydrates 9.8 g
- Sugar 4.9 g
- Protein 20.9 g
- Cholesterol 320 mg

Delicious Beef Barbacoa

Preparation Time: 10 minutes
Cooking Time: 8 hours
Serve: 8

Ingredients:

- 3 lbs chuck roast, trimmed and cut into cubes
- 3 chipotles in adobo, chopped
- 3 garlic cloves, minced
- 1/2 tsp ground cloves
- 1 tbsp onion powder
- 1 tbsp dried oregano
- 1 tbsp ground cumin
- 3 tbsp apple cider vinegar
- 1/4 cup lime juice
- 4 oz can green chilies, diced
- 1/2 cup beef broth
- Pepper
- Salt

Directions:

1. Add all ingredients into the pot stir well to combine. Cover pot with foil.
2. Place pot on the wire rack then places the rack at a low position in the toaster oven.
3. Select the slow cook mode and set the time to 8 hours. Press starts.
4. Shred meat using a fork and season with pepper and salt.
5. Stir well and serve.

Nutritional Value (Amount per Serving):

- Calories 389
- Fat 14.9 g
- Carbohydrates 3.3 g
- Sugar 5 g
- Protein 20.9 g
- Cholesterol 320 mg

Easy Steak Bites

Preparation Time: 10 minutes
Cooking Time: 8 hours
Serve: 4

Ingredients:

- 3 lbs round steak, cut into 1-inch cubes
- 1 tsp garlic powder
- 1 tbsp onion, minced
- 1/2 cup chicken broth
- 1/2 tsp black pepper
- 4 tbsp butter, sliced
- 1/2 tsp salt

Directions:

1. Place meat cubes into the pot and pour broth over the meat.
2. Sprinkle with garlic powder, onion, pepper, and salt.
3. Place butter slices on top of the meat. Cover pot with foil.
4. Place pot on the wire rack then places the rack at a low position in the toaster oven.
5. Select the slow cook mode and set the time to 8 hours. Press starts.
6. Stir well and serve.

Nutritional Value (Amount per Serving):

- Calories 845
- Fat 44.4 g
- Carbohydrates 1 g
- Sugar 0.4 g
- Protein 103.6 g
- Cholesterol 320 mg

Italian Beef Roast

Preparation Time: 10 minutes
Cooking Time: 8 hours
Serve: 8

Ingredients:

- 2 1/2 lbs beef round roast
- 1/2 tsp marjoram
- 1/2 tsp thyme
- 1 tsp basil
- 1/4 tsp black pepper
- 1/2 cup red wine
- 1/2 cup chicken broth
- 1 small onion, sliced
- 1 tsp kosher salt

Directions:

1. In a small bowl, mix all spices and rub all over beef roast.
2. Place roast in the pot and top with onion.
3. Pour broth and red wine into the pot. Cover pot with foil.
4. Place pot on the wire rack then places the rack at a low position in the toaster oven.
5. Select the slow cook mode and set the time to 2 hours. Press starts.
6. Shred meat using a fork and stir well and serve.

Nutritional Value (Amount per Serving):

- Calories 284
- Fat 11 g
- Carbohydrates 1.4 g
- Sugar 0.5 g
- Protein 39.3 g
- Cholesterol 122 mg

Rosemary Lemon Lamb Roast

Preparation Time: 10 minutes
Cooking Time: 4 hours
Serve: 6

Ingredients:

- 4 lbs lamb leg
- 4 tbsp rosemary
- 1 tbsp garlic, sliced
- 1 fresh lemon juice
- 1 tbsp olive oil
- Pepper
- Salt

Directions:

1. Place meat into the pot and top with remaining ingredients. Cover pot with foil.
2. Place pot on the wire rack then places the rack at a low position in the toaster oven.
3. Select the slow cook mode and set the time to 4 hours. Press starts.
4. Slice and serve.

Nutritional Value (Amount per Serving):

- Calories 576
- Fat 22.9 g
- Carbohydrates 2.2 g
- Sugar 0.2 g
- Protein 85.5 g
- Cholesterol 263 mg

Meatloaf

Preparation Time: 10 minutes
Cooking Time: 40 minutes
Serve: 8

Ingredients:

- 2 eggs
- 2 lbs ground beef
- 2 tsp Italian seasoning
- 1/4 cup pesto
- 1/2 cup parmesan cheese, grated
- 1/2 cup marinara sauce
- 1 cup cottage cheese
- 1 lb mozzarella cheese, cut into cubes
- 1 tsp salt

Directions:

1. Preheat the cosori air fryer toaster oven to 400 F.
2. Add all ingredients into the large bowl and mix until well combined.
3. Transfer bowl mixture into the greased loaf pan.
4. Place loaf pan on the wire rack, then place the rack at mid-position in the toaster oven.
5. Select the bake mode and set the time to 40 minutes. Press starts.
6. Serve and enjoy.

Nutritional Value (Amount per Serving):

- Calories 299
- Fat 11.5 g
- Carbohydrates 3.8 g
- Sugar 1.7 g
- Protein 43 g
- Cholesterol 124 mg

Meatballs

Preparation Time: 10 minutes
Cooking Time: 20 minutes
Serve: 6

Ingredients:

- 1 egg
- 2 lbs ground beef
- 1/4 cup fresh parsley, minced
- 1/2 tsp allspice
- 1 tsp oregano
- 1 tsp cinnamon
- 2 tsp cumin
- 2 tsp coriander
- 1 tsp garlic, minced
- 1 small onion, grated
- 1 tbsp fresh mint, chopped
- 1 tsp paprika
- 1/4 tsp pepper
- 1/2 tsp salt

Directions:

1. Preheat the cosori air fryer toaster oven to 400 F.
2. Add all ingredients into the bowl and mix until well combined.
3. Make small balls from the meat mixture and place them onto the baking sheet.
4. Place baking sheet on the wire rack, then place the rack at mid-position in the toaster oven.
5. Select the bake mode and set the time to 20 minutes. Press starts.
6. Serve and enjoy.

Nutritional Value (Amount per Serving):

- Calories 291
- Fat 15.7 g
- Carbohydrates 2.7 g
- Sugar 0.7 g
- Protein 32.2 g
- Cholesterol 128 mg

Flavors Pork Cacciatore

Preparation Time: 10 minutes
Cooking Time: 6 hours
Serve: 6

Ingredients:

- 1 1/2 lbs pork chops
- 3 tbsp tomato paste
- 14 oz can tomato, diced
- 2 cups mushrooms, sliced
- 1 cup beef broth
- 1 garlic clove, minced
- 1 tsp dried oregano
- 2 tbsp olive oil
- 1 small onion, diced
- 1/4 tsp pepper
- 1/2 tsp salt

Directions:

1. Heat oil in a pan over medium-high heat.
2. Add pork chops in the pan and cook until brown.
3. Transfer pork chops into the pot. Pour remaining ingredients over the pork chops. Cover pot with foil.
4. Place pot on the wire rack then places the rack at a low position in the toaster oven.
5. Select the slow cook mode and set the time to 6 hours. Press starts.
6. Serve and enjoy.

Nutritional Value (Amount per Serving):

- Calories 441
- Fat 33.2 g
- Carbohydrates 7.3 g
- Sugar 4.3 g
- Protein 28.2 g
- Cholesterol 98 mg

Greek Pork Roast

Preparation Time: 10 minutes

Cooking Time: 6 hours

Serve: 8

Ingredients:

- 2 lbs lean pork roast, boneless
- 1 tsp dried basil
- 1 tsp garlic powder
- 1 tbsp parsley
- 1/2 cup parmesan cheese, grated
- 28 oz can tomato, diced
- 1 tsp dried oregano
- Pepper
- Salt

Directions:

1. Add the meat into the pot.
2. Mix together tomatoes, oregano, basil, garlic powder, parsley, cheese, pepper, and salt and pour over meat. Cover pot with foil.
3. Place pot on the wire rack then places the rack at a low position in the toaster oven.
4. Select the slow cook mode and set the time to 6 hours. Press starts.
5. Stir well and serve.

Nutritional Value (Amount per Serving):

- Calories 239
- Fat 8.5 g
- Carbohydrates 5.7 g
- Sugar 3.5 g
- Protein 33.9 g
- Cholesterol 94 mg

Simple Lamb Patties

Preparation Time: 10 minutes
Cooking Time: 15 minutes
Serve: 4

Ingredients:

- 1 lb ground lamb
- 1/4 tsp pepper
- 1/4 tsp cayenne
- 1/2 tsp ground allspice
- 1 tsp ground cumin
- 1/4 cup fresh parsley, chopped
- 1/4 cup onion, minced
- 1 tbsp garlic, minced
- 1 tsp ground coriander
- 1 tsp kosher salt

Directions:

1. Preheat the cosori air fryer toaster oven to 400 F.
2. Add all ingredients into the bowl and mix until well combined.
3. Make patties from the mixture and place them onto the baking sheet.
4. Place baking sheet on the wire rack, then place the rack at mid-position in the toaster oven.
5. Select the bake mode and set the time to 15 minutes. Press starts.
6. Serve and enjoy.

Nutritional Value (Amount per Serving):

- Calories 223
- Fat 8.5 g
- Carbohydrates 2.6 g
- Sugar 0.4 g
- Protein 32.3 g
- Cholesterol 102 mg

Salsa Pork

Preparation Time: 10 minutes

Cooking Time: 3 hours

Serve: 8

Ingredients:

- 8 pork chops
- 1/4 cup fresh lime juice
- 1/2 tsp ground cumin
- 1/2 cup salsa
- 3 tbsp olive oil
- 1 tsp garlic powder
- Pepper
- Salt

Directions:

1. Heat oil in a pan over medium-high heat.
2. Add pork chops in a pan and cook until browned.
3. Place pork chops into the pot. Pour remaining ingredients over pork chops. Cover pot with foil.
4. Place pot on the wire rack then places the rack at a low position in the toaster oven.
5. Select the slow cook mode and set the time to 3 hours. Press starts.
6. Stir well and serve.

Nutritional Value (Amount per Serving):

- Calories 307
- Fat 25.2 g
- Carbohydrates 1.5 g
- Sugar 0.6 g
- Protein 18.3 g
- Cholesterol 1.5 mg

Meatballs

Preparation Time: 10 minutes
Cooking Time: 10 minutes
Serve: 4

Ingredients:

- 1 egg
- 1 lb ground beef
- 1/4 cup onion, chopped
- 1/2 cup cheddar cheese, shredded
- 1 1/2 tbsp taco seasoning
- 1 tbsp garlic, minced
- 1/4 cup cilantro, chopped
- Pepper
- Salt

Directions:

1. Preheat the cosori air fryer toaster oven to 390 F.
2. Add ground beef and remaining ingredients into the bowl and mix until well combined.
3. Make small balls from the meat mixture and place them onto the baking sheet.
4. Place baking sheet on the wire rack, then place the rack at the mid position in the toaster oven.
5. Select the bake mode and set the time to 10 minutes. Press starts.
6. Serve and enjoy.

Nutritional Value (Amount per Serving):

- Calories 293
- Fat 13 g
- Carbohydrates 1.9 g
- Sugar 0.5 g
- Protein 39.7 g
- Cholesterol 158 mg

Beef Burger Patties

Preparation Time: 10 minutes

Cooking Time: 12 minutes

Serve: 4

Ingredients:

- 1 lb ground beef
- 1/2 tsp onion powder
- 1/4 tsp chili powder
- 1/2 tsp garlic powder
- Pepper
- Salt

Directions:

1. Preheat the cosori air fryer toaster oven to 350 F.
2. Add all ingredients into the bowl and mix until well combined.
3. Make patties from the meat mixture and place them onto the baking sheet.
4. Place baking sheet on the wire rack, then place the rack at mid-position in the toaster oven.
5. Select the bake mode and set the time to 12 minutes. Press starts.
6. Serve and enjoy.

Nutritional Value (Amount per Serving):

- Calories 213
- Fat 7.1 g
- Carbohydrates 0.6 g
- Sugar 0.2 g
- Protein 34.5 g
- Cholesterol 101 mg

Garlic Beef Roast

Preparation Time: 10 minutes
Cooking Time: 8 hours
Serve: 6

Ingredients:

- 2 lbs top round beef roast
- 2 cups beef broth
- 1/2 cup red wine
- 1 tsp chili flakes
- 1 tbsp Italian seasoning
- 8 garlic cloves, minced
- 1 onion, sliced
- Pepper
- Salt

Directions:

1. Season meat with pepper and salt and place into the pot. Pour remaining ingredients over meat. Cover pot with foil.
2. Place pot on the wire rack then places the rack at a low position in the toaster oven.
3. Select the slow cook mode and set the time to 8 hours. Press starts.
4. Stir well and serve.

Nutritional Value (Amount per Serving):

- Calories 231
- Fat 6.7 g
- Carbohydrates 4 g
- Sugar 1.4 g
- Protein 35.8 g
- Cholesterol 76 mg

Meatballs

Preparation Time: 10 minutes
Cooking Time: 20 minutes
Serve: 4

Ingredients:

- 1 egg
- 1 lb ground lamb
- 1 tsp ground cumin
- 2 tsp fresh oregano, chopped
- 2 tbsp fresh parsley, chopped
- 3 tbsp olive oil
- 1 tbsp garlic, minced
- 1/4 tsp pepper
- 1 tsp kosher salt

Directions:

1. Preheat the cosori air fryer toaster oven to 390 F.
2. Line baking sheet with parchment paper.
3. Add all ingredients except oil into the bowl and mix until well combined.
4. Make small balls from the meat mixture and place them onto the baking sheet. Drizzle oil over meatballs.
5. Place baking sheet on the wire rack, then place the rack at mid-position in the toaster oven.
6. Select the bake mode and set the time to 20 minutes. Press starts.
7. Serve and enjoy.

Nutritional Value (Amount per Serving):

- Calories 325
- Fat 20.2 g
- Carbohydrates 1.7 g
- Sugar 0.2 g
- Protein 33.6 g
- Cholesterol 143 mg

Greek Pork Roast

Preparation Time: 10 minutes
Cooking Time: 6 hours
Serve: 8

Ingredients:

- 2 lbs pork roast, boneless
- 1 tsp dried oregano
- 1 tsp dried basil
- 1 tsp garlic powder
- 1/2 cup parmesan cheese, grated
- 28 oz can tomato, diced
- Pepper
- Salt

Directions:

1. Add the meat into the pot.
2. Mix together tomatoes, oregano, basil, garlic powder, parsley, cheese, pepper, and salt and pour over meat. Cover pot with foil.
3. Place pot on the wire rack then places the rack at a low position in the toaster oven.
4. Select the slow cook mode and set the time to 6 hours. Press starts.
5. Stir well and serve.

Nutritional Value (Amount per Serving):

- Calories 237
- Fat 8.4 g
- Carbohydrates 5.7 g
- Sugar 3.5 g
- Protein 33.7 g
- Cholesterol 94 mg

Garlic Lamb Roast

Preparation Time: 10 minutes

Cooking Time: 8 hours

Serve: 8

Ingredients:

- 4 lbs lamb roast, boneless
- 1/2 tsp marjoram
- 1/2 tsp thyme
- 5 garlic cloves, cut into slivers
- 1 tsp oregano
- 1/4 tsp pepper
- 2 tsp salt

Directions:

1. Using a sharp knife make small cuts all over lamb roast then insert garlic slivers into the cuts.
2. In a small bowl, mix marjoram, thyme, oregano, pepper, and salt and rub all over lamb roast.
3. Place lamb roast into the pot. Cover pot with foil.
4. Place pot on the wire rack then places the rack at a low position in the toaster oven.
5. Select the slow cook mode and set the time to 8 hours. Press starts.
6. Stir well and serve.

Nutritional Value (Amount per Serving):

- Calories 605
- Fat 48.2 g
- Carbohydrates 0.7 g
- Sugar 0 g
- Protein 38.3 g
- Cholesterol 161 mg

Baked Lamb Patties

Preparation Time: 10 minutes

Cooking Time: 15 minutes

Serve: 4

Ingredients:

- 1 lb ground lamb
- 1/2 tsp ground allspice
- 1 tbsp garlic, minced
- 1 tsp ground coriander
- 1 tsp ground cumin
- 1/4 cup onion, minced
- 1/4 tsp cayenne
- 1/4 tsp pepper
- 1 tsp kosher salt

Directions:

1. Preheat the cosori air fryer toaster oven to 390 F.
2. Add all ingredients into the bowl and mix until well combined.
3. Make patties from the meat mixture and place them onto the baking sheet.
4. Place baking sheet on the wire rack, then place the rack at mid-position in the toaster oven.
5. Select the bake mode and set the time to 15 minutes. Press starts.
6. Serve and enjoy.

Nutritional Value (Amount per Serving):

- Calories 223
- Fat 8.5 g
- Carbohydrates 2.6 g
- Sugar 0.4 g
- Protein 32.3 g
- Cholesterol 102 mg

Meatballs

Preparation Time: 10 minutes

Cooking Time: 15 minutes

Serve: 4

Ingredients:

- 1 lb ground pork
- 1/2 tsp ground cumin
- 1/2 tsp coriander
- 1 tsp onion powder
- 1 tsp paprika
- 1 tsp garlic powder
- Pepper
- Salt

Directions:

1. Preheat the cosori air fryer toaster oven to 390 F.
2. Add all ingredients into the bowl and mix until well combined.
3. Make small balls from the meat mixture and place them onto the baking sheet.
4. Place baking sheet on the wire rack, then place the rack at mid-position in the toaster oven.
5. Select the bake mode and set the time to 15 minutes. Press starts.
6. Serve and enjoy.

Nutritional Value (Amount per Serving):

- Calories 170
- Fat 4.1 g
- Carbohydrates 1.5 g
- Sugar 0.4 g
- Protein 30 g
- Cholesterol 83 mg

Baked Lamb Chops

Preparation Time: 10 minutes
Cooking Time: 30 minutes
Serve: 4

Ingredients:

- 4 lamb chops
- 1 tsp garlic powder
- 1 tsp ground cinnamon
- 1 1/2 tsp ginger
- 1/4 cup brown sugar
- Pepper
- Salt

Directions:

1. Preheat the cosori air fryer toaster oven to 375 F.
2. Add garlic powder, cinnamon, ginger, brown sugar, pepper, and salt into the zip-lock bag and mix well.
3. Add lamb chops in a zip-lock bag. Seal bag and place in the refrigerator for 2 hours.
4. Place marinated lamb chops on a baking sheet.
5. Place baking sheet on the wire rack, then place the rack at mid-position in the toaster oven.
6. Select the bake mode and set the time to 30 minutes. Press starts.
7. Serve and enjoy.

Nutritional Value (Amount per Serving):

- Calories 650
- Fat 24.1 g
- Carbohydrates 10.5 g
- Sugar 9 g
- Protein 92.1 g
- Cholesterol 294 mg

Chapter 5: Fish & Seafood

Flavorful Crab Cakes

Preparation Time: 10 minutes

Cooking Time: 10 minutes

Serve: 4

Ingredients:

- 8 oz lump crab
- 2 tbsp mayonnaise
- 2 tbsp green onion, chopped
- 1/4 cup bell pepper, chopped
- 1 tsp old bay seasoning
- 1 tbsp Dijon mustard
- 2 tbsp breadcrumbs
- Pepper
- Salt

Directions:

1. Preheat the cosori air fryer toaster oven to 370 F.
2. Add lump crab and remaining ingredients into the bowl and mix until well combined.
3. Make patties from the mixture and place them into the fry basket.
4. Place the fry basket on the wire rack, then place the rack at the top position in the toaster oven.
5. Select the air fry mode and set the time to 10 minutes. Press starts.
6. Serve and enjoy.

Nutritional Value (Amount per Serving):

- Calories 156
- Fat 14.2 g
- Carbohydrates 6.7 g
- Sugar 1.5 g
- Protein 11.6 g
- Cholesterol 34 mg

Garlic Butter Shrimp

Preparation Time: 10 minutes

Cooking Time: 6 minutes

Serve: 4

Ingredients:

- 12 shrimp, peeled and deveined
- 3 tbsp butter, melted
- 4 garlic cloves, minced
- Pepper
- Salt

Directions:

1. Preheat the cosori air fryer toaster oven to 360 F.
2. In a bowl, add shrimp, garlic, butter, pepper, and salt and mix well. Set aside for 15 minutes.
3. Place shrimp in a fry basket.
4. Place the fry basket on the wire rack, then place the rack at the top position in the toaster oven.
5. Select the air fry mode and set the time to 6 minutes. Press starts.
6. Serve and enjoy.

Nutritional Value (Amount per Serving):

- Calories 99
- Fat 8.9 g
- Carbohydrates 1 g
- Sugar 0 g
- Protein 4 g
- Cholesterol 58 mg

Curried Fish Fillets

Preparation Time: 10 minutes
Cooking Time: 10 minutes
Serve: 2

Ingredients:

- 2 cod fillets
- 1/4 tsp curry powder
- 1 tbsp butter, melted
- 1/8 tsp garlic powder
- 1/8 tsp paprika
- 1/8 tsp sea salt

Directions:

1. Preheat the cosori air fryer toaster oven to 360 F.
2. In a small bowl, mix curry powder, garlic powder, paprika, and salt and set aside.
3. Place cod fillets into the fry basket. Brush fish fillets with butter and sprinkle with spice mixture.
4. Place the fry basket on the wire rack, then place the rack at the top position in the toaster oven.
5. Select the air fry mode and set the time to 10 minutes. Press starts.
6. Serve and enjoy.

Nutritional Value (Amount per Serving):

- Calories 143
- Fat 6.8 g
- Carbohydrates 0.4 g
- Sugar 0.1 g
- Protein 20.2 g
- Cholesterol 70 mg

Crispy Shrimp

Preparation Time: 10 minutes
Cooking Time: 10 minutes
Serve: 4

Ingredients:

- 1 lb shrimp, peeled and deveined
- 1/2 tsp Cajun seasoning
- 1/2 tsp garlic, minced
- 1 tbsp olive oil
- Pepper
- Salt

Directions:

1. Preheat the cosori air fryer toaster oven to 350 F.
2. Add shrimp, oil, Cajun seasoning, garlic, pepper, and salt into the bowl. Toss well.
3. Add shrimp into the fry basket.
4. Place the fry basket on the wire rack, then place the rack at the top position in the toaster oven.
5. Select the air fry mode and set the time to 10 minutes. Press starts.
6. Serve and enjoy.

Nutritional Value (Amount per Serving):

- Calories 166
- Fat 5.4 g
- Carbohydrates 2 g
- Sugar 0 g
- Protein 25.9 g
- Cholesterol 239 mg

Simple Salmon Patties

Preparation Time: 10 minutes

Cooking Time: 7 minutes

Serve: 2

Ingredients:

- 1 egg
- 8 oz salmon fillet, minced
- 1/8 tsp lemon zest
- 1/4 tsp garlic powder
- Pepper
- Salt

Directions:

1. Preheat the cosori air fryer toaster oven to 390 F.
2. In a bowl, mix together salmon, garlic powder, lemon zest, egg, and salt until well combined.
3. Make two patties from the salmon mixture and place them in a fry basket.
4. Place the fry basket on the wire rack, then place the rack at the top position in the toaster oven.
5. Select the air fry mode and set the time to 7 minutes. Press starts.
6. Serve and enjoy.

Nutritional Value (Amount per Serving):

- Calories 191
- Fat 9.3 g
- Carbohydrates 3.1 g
- Sugar 1 g
- Protein 25.2 g
- Cholesterol 132 mg

Salmon with Carrots

Preparation Time: 10 minutes
Cooking Time: 20 minutes
Serve: 4

Ingredients:

- 1 lb salmon, cut into four pieces
- 2 tbsp butter, melted
- 2 cups baby carrots
- Salt

Directions:

1. Preheat the cosori air fryer toaster oven to 425 F.
2. Place salmon pieces onto the baking sheet.
3. In a bowl, toss together baby carrots and olive oil.
4. Arrange carrot around the salmon. Season with salt.
5. Place baking sheet on the wire rack, then place the rack at mid-position in the toaster oven.
6. Select the bake mode and set the time to 20 minutes. Press starts.
7. Serve and enjoy.

Nutritional Value (Amount per Serving):

- Calories 225
- Fat 14.1 g
- Carbohydrates 3.5 g
- Sugar 2 g
- Protein 22.3 g
- Cholesterol 50 mg

Herb Salmon

Preparation Time: 10 minutes
Cooking Time: 15 minutes
Serve: 4

Ingredients:

- 1 lbs salmon, cut into pieces
- 1/4 tsp dried basil
- 1 tbsp olive oil
- 1/2 tbsp dried rosemary
- Pepper
- Salt

Directions:

1. Preheat the cosori air fryer toaster oven to 400 F.
2. Place salmon pieces into the baking dish.
3. In a small bowl, mix together olive oil, basil, and rosemary.
4. Brush salmon with oil mixture.
5. Place baking dish on the wire rack, then place the rack at mid-position in the toaster oven.
6. Select the bake mode and set the time to 15 minutes. Press starts.
7. Serve and enjoy.

Nutritional Value (Amount per Serving):

- Calories 182
- Fat 10.6 g
- Carbohydrates 0.3 g
- Sugar 0 g
- Protein 22 g
- Cholesterol 50 mg

Lemon White Fish Fillets

Preparation Time: 10 minutes
Cooking Time: 30 minutes
Serve: 1

Ingredients:

- 8 oz frozen white fish fillet
- 1 tbsp lemon juice
- 1 tbsp fresh parsley, chopped
- 1 tbsp roasted bell pepper, diced
- 1/2 tsp Italian seasoning
- 1 1/2 tbsp butter, melted

Directions:

1. Preheat the cosori air fryer toaster oven to 400 F.
2. Place a fish fillet on a baking sheet. Drizzle butter and lemon juice over fish.
3. Sprinkle with Italian seasoning. Top with bell pepper and parsley.
4. Place baking sheet on the wire rack, then place the rack at the mid position in the toaster oven.
5. Select the bake mode and set the time to 30 minutes. Press starts.
6. Serve and enjoy.

Nutritional Value (Amount per Serving):

- Calories 355
- Fat 18.8 g
- Carbohydrates 1.3 g
- Sugar 0.8 g
- Protein 46.8 g
- Cholesterol 47 mg

Greek Salmon

Preparation Time: 10 minutes

Cooking Time: 10 minutes

Serve: 4

Ingredients:

- 24 oz salmon, cut into pieces
- 1 tbsp yogurt
- 1 tsp lemon zest
- 2 tbsp lemon juice
- 2 tbsp olive oil
- 1 tsp oregano
- 1 garlic clove, grated
- 1/4 tsp pepper
- 1/4 tsp salt

Directions:

1. Preheat the cosori air fryer toaster oven to 400 F.
2. Add all ingredients except salmon in a baking dish and mix well.
3. Add salmon and coat well and let it sit for 30 minutes.
4. Place baking dish on the wire rack, then place the rack at mid-position in the toaster oven.
5. Select the bake mode and set the time to 10 minutes. Press starts.
6. Serve and enjoy.

Nutritional Value (Amount per Serving):

- Calories 292
- Fat 17.7 g
- Carbohydrates 1.1 g
- Sugar 0.5 g
- Protein 33.4 g
- Cholesterol 75 mg

Italian Salmon

Preparation Time: 10 minute
Cooking Time: 20 minutes
Serve: 5

Ingredients:

- 1 3/4 lbs salmon fillet
- 1/3 cup pesto
- 1 tbsp fresh dill, chopped
- 1/4 cup capers
- 1/3 cup artichoke hearts
- 1/4 cup sun-dried tomatoes, drained
- 1/4 cup olives, pitted and chopped
- 1 tsp paprika
- 1/4 tsp salt

Directions:

1. Preheat the cosori air fryer toaster oven to 400 F.
2. Line baking sheet with parchment paper.
3. Arrange salmon fillet on a prepared baking sheet and sprinkle with paprika and salt.
4. Add remaining ingredients on top of salmon.
5. Place baking sheet on the wire rack, then place the rack at mid-position in the toaster oven.
6. Select the bake mode and set the time to 20 minutes. Press starts.
7. Serve and enjoy.

Nutritional Value (Amount per Serving):

- Calories 228
- Fat 10.7 g
- Carbohydrates 2.6 g
- Sugar 0.4 g
- Protein 31.6 g
- Cholesterol 70 mg

Baked Tilapia with Feta Cheese

Preparation Time: 10 minutes

Cooking Time: 17 minutes

Serve: 2

Ingredients:

- 1/2 lb tilapia fillets
- 2 oz feta cheese, crumbled
- 2/3 cup tomatoes, chopped
- 1/3 cup fresh parsley, chopped
- 1 tsp olive oil
- 1 1/2 tbsp garlic, minced
- Pepper
- Salt

Directions:

1. Preheat the cosori air fryer toaster oven to 400 F.
2. In a bowl, mix tomatoes, garlic, feta, parsley, and oil.
3. Spray tilapia fillets with cooking spray and season with pepper and salt.
4. Place tilapia fillets on a baking dish and top and with tomato mixture.
5. Place baking dish on the wire rack, then place the rack at mid-position in the toaster oven.
6. Select the bake mode and set the time to 17 minutes. Press starts.
7. Serve and enjoy.

Nutritional Value (Amount per Serving):

- Calories 212
- Fat 9.6 g
- Carbohydrates 6.2 g
- Sugar 2.9 g
- Protein 26.4 g
- Cholesterol 80 mg

Baked Lemon Cod

Preparation Time: 10 minutes
Cooking Time: 10 minutes
Serve: 2

Ingredients:

- 1 lb cod fillets, rinsed and pat dry
- 1 tbsp fresh parsley, chopped
- 1 1/2 tbsp olive oil
- 1/8 tsp cayenne
- 1 tbsp fresh lemon juice
- 1/4 tsp salt

Directions:

1. Preheat the cosori air fryer toaster oven to 400 F.
2. Place fish fillets onto the baking sheet.
3. Drizzle with oil and lemon juice and season with cayenne and salt.
4. Place baking sheet on the wire rack, then place the rack at mid-position in the toaster oven.
5. Select the bake mode and set the time to 10 minutes. Press starts.
6. Garnish with parsley and serve.

Nutritional Value (Amount per Serving):

- Calories 275
- Fat 12.6 g
- Carbohydrates 0.3 g
- Sugar 0.2 g
- Protein 40.6 g
- Cholesterol 111 mg

Lemon Pepper Fish Fillets

Preparation Time: 10 minutes

Cooking Time: 12 minutes

Serve: 4

Ingredients:

- 4 basa fish fillets
- 1/4 tsp lemon pepper seasoning
- 4 tbsp fresh lemon juice
- 8 tsp olive oil
- 1/2 tsp garlic powder
- Pepper
- Salt

Directions:

1. Preheat the cosori air fryer toaster oven to 425 F.
2. Place fish fillets in a baking dish.
3. Pour oil and lemon juice over fish fillets. Sprinkle remaining ingredients.
4. Place baking dish on the wire rack, then place the rack at mid-position in the toaster oven.
5. Select the bake mode and set the time to 12 minutes. Press starts.
6. Serve and enjoy.

Nutritional Value (Amount per Serving):

- Calories 308
- Fat 21.4 g
- Carbohydrates 5.4 g
- Sugar 3.4 g
- Protein 24.1 g
- Cholesterol 0 mg

Delicious Catfish Fillets

Preparation Time: 10 minutes
Cooking Time: 15 minutes
Serve: 4

Ingredients:

- 1 lb catfish fillets
- 3/4 tsp chili powder
- 1 tsp crushed red pepper
- 2 tsp onion powder
- 1 tbsp dried oregano, crushed
- 1/2 tsp ground cumin
- Pepper
- Salt

Directions:

1. Preheat the cosori air fryer toaster oven to 350 F.
2. In a small bowl, mix cumin, chili powder, crushed pepper, onion powder, oregano, pepper, and salt.
3. Rub fish fillets with the spice mixture and place them in a baking dish.
4. Place baking dish on the wire rack, then place the rack at mid-position in the toaster oven.
5. Select the bake mode and set the time to 15 minutes. Press starts.
6. Serve and enjoy.

Nutritional Value (Amount per Serving):

- Calories 165
- Fat 9 g
- Carbohydrates 2.4 g
- Sugar 0.6 g
- Protein 18 g
- Cholesterol 53 mg

Flavorful Halibut

Preparation Time: 10 minutes
Cooking Time: 12 minutes
Serve: 4

Ingredients:

- 1 lb halibut fillets
- 1/2 tsp paprika
- 1/4 cup olive oil
- 1/4 tsp garlic powder
- Pepper
- Salt

Directions:

1. Preheat the cosori air fryer toaster oven to 425 F.
2. Place fish fillets in a baking dish.
3. In a small bowl, mix oil, garlic powder, paprika, pepper, and salt.
4. Brush fish fillets with oil mixture.
5. Place baking dish on the wire rack, then place the rack at mid-position in the toaster oven.
6. Select the bake mode and set the time to 12 minutes. Press starts.
7. Serve and enjoy.

Nutritional Value (Amount per Serving):

- Calories 270
- Fat 15.3 g
- Carbohydrates 0.3 g
- Sugar 0.1 g
- Protein 30.8 g
- Cholesterol 53 mg

Chapter 6: Vegetable & Side Dishes

Cheesy Eggplant Gratin

Preparation Time: 10 minutes
Cooking Time: 45 minutes
Serve: 6

Ingredients:

- 2 lbs eggplant, cut into 1/2-inch slices
- 1/3 lb feta cheese, crumbled
- 2 tbsp olive oil
- 2 onions, sliced
- 3/4 cup heavy cream
- 6 tbsp cheddar cheese, shredded
- Pepper
- Salt

Directions:

1. Preheat the cosori air fryer toaster oven to 390 F.
2. Brush eggplants slices with oil and place in baking dish. Season with salt.
3. Place baking dish on the wire rack, then place the rack at mid-position in the toaster oven.
4. Select the bake mode and set the time to 15 minutes. Press starts.
5. Sprinkle fried onion over eggplants then sprinkle with cheddar cheese and feta cheese. Pour cream over eggplant.
6. Place dish in the toaster oven and bake for 30 minutes more.
7. Serve and enjoy.

Nutritional Value (Amount per Serving):

- Calories 240
- Fat 18.3 g
- Carbohydrates 14.2 g
- Sugar 7.2 g
- Protein 7.7 g
- Cholesterol 50 mg

Baked Creamy Cauliflower

Preparation Time: 10 minutes

Cooking Time: 20 minutes

Serve: 4

Ingredients:

- 1 cauliflower head, cut into florets
- 2 tbsp fresh lemon juice
- 1/2 cup cheddar cheese, shredded
- 1/2 cup mayonnaise
- 2 tsp Dijon mustard
- 1/4 cup sour cream

Directions:

1. Preheat the cosori air fryer toaster oven to 375 F.
2. Spread cauliflower florets onto the baking sheet.
3. Place baking sheet on the wire rack, then place the rack at mid-position in the toaster oven.
4. Select the bake mode and set the time to 10 minutes. Press starts.
5. In a bowl, mix together cauliflower, lemon juice, cheese, mayonnaise, mustard, and sour cream and pour into the casserole dish and bake for 10 minutes more.
6. Serve and enjoy.

Nutritional Value (Amount per Serving):

- Calories 222
- Fat 17.7 g
- Carbohydrates 11.6 g
- Sugar 3.7 g
- Protein 5.7 g
- Cholesterol 29 mg

Easy Baked Carrots

Preparation Time: 10 minutes
Cooking Time: 30 minutes
Serve: 4

Ingredients:

- 25 baby carrots
- 6 tbsp butter, melted
- 1 tsp cinnamon
- 1 tbsp maple syrup
- Pepper
- Salt

Directions:

1. Preheat the cosori air fryer toaster oven to 390 F.
2. Arrange carrots in the baking dish. Pour butter over carrots.
3. Sprinkle cinnamon, pepper, and salt over carrots.
4. Place baking dish on the wire rack, then place the rack at mid-position in the toaster oven.
5. Select the bake mode and set the time to 30 minutes. Press starts.
6. Drizzle maple syrup over carrots and serve.

Nutritional Value (Amount per Serving):

- Calories 176
- Fat 17.4 g
- Carbohydrates 5.7 g
- Sugar 3 g
- Protein 0.6 g
- Cholesterol 46 mg

Roasted Broccoli

Preparation Time: 10 minutes
Cooking Time: 20 minutes
Serve: 6

Ingredients:

- 4 cups broccoli florets
- 1 tsp Italian seasoning
- 3 tbsp olive oil
- 1/2 tsp garlic powder
- 1/2 tsp pepper
- 1 tsp salt

Directions:

1. Preheat the cosori air fryer toaster oven to 400 F.
2. Spread broccoli onto the baking sheet and drizzle with oil and season with garlic powder, Italian seasoning, pepper, and salt.
3. Place baking sheet on the wire rack, then place the rack at mid-position in the toaster oven.
4. Select the bake mode and set the time to 20 minutes. Press starts.
5. Serve and enjoy.

Nutritional Value (Amount per Serving):

- Calories 84
- Fat 7.4 g
- Carbohydrates 4.4 g
- Sugar 11 g
- Protein 1.8 g
- Cholesterol 1 mg

Healthy Cauliflower & Tomatoes

Preparation Time: 10 minutes

Cooking Time: 20 minutes

Serve: 4

Ingredients:

- 4 cups cauliflower florets
- 2 garlic cloves, sliced
- 1 tbsp capers, drained
- 3 tbsp olive oil
- 1/2 cup cherry tomatoes, halved
- Pepper
- Salt

Directions:

1. Preheat the cosori air fryer toaster oven to 450 F.
2. In a bowl, toss tomatoes, cauliflower, oil, garlic, capers, pepper, and salt and spread on a baking sheet.
3. Place baking sheet on the wire rack, then place the rack at mid-position in the toaster oven.
4. Select the bake mode and set the time to 20 minutes. Press starts.
5. Serve and enjoy.

Nutritional Value (Amount per Serving):

- Calories 123
- Fat 10.7 g
- Carbohydrates 6.9 g
- Sugar 3 g
- Protein 2.4 g
- Cholesterol 0 mg

Greek Mushrooms & Cauliflower

Preparation Time: 10 minutes
Cooking Time: 20 minutes
Serve: 6

Ingredients:

- 1 lb mushrooms, cleaned
- 1 tbsp Italian seasoning
- 2 tbsp olive oil
- 8 garlic cloves, peeled
- 2 cups cherry tomatoes
- 2 cups cauliflower florets
- Pepper
- Salt

Directions:

1. Preheat the cosori air fryer toaster oven to 400 F.
2. Add cauliflower, mushrooms, Italian seasoning, olive oil, garlic, tomatoes, pepper, and salt into the bowl and toss well.
3. Transfer cauliflower and mushroom mixture onto a baking sheet.
4. Place baking sheet on the wire rack, then place the rack at mid-position in the toaster oven.
5. Select the bake mode and set the time to 20 minutes. Press starts.
6. Serve and enjoy.

Nutritional Value (Amount per Serving):

- Calories 90
- Fat 5.8 g
- Carbohydrates 8.5 g
- Sugar 3.9 g
- Protein 3.9 g
- Cholesterol 2 mg

Baked Brussels Sprouts

Preparation Time: 10 minutes
Cooking Time: 15 minutes
Serve: 4

Ingredients:

- 1 lb Brussels sprouts, halved
- 1/2 tsp garlic powder
- 1/8 tsp paprika
- 2 tbsp olive oil
- 1/8 tsp cayenne
- Pepper
- Salt

Directions:

1. Preheat the cosori air fryer toaster oven to 400 F.
2. Add Brussels sprouts, paprika, garlic powder, cayenne, oil, pepper, and salt into the bowl and toss well.
3. Spread Brussels sprouts onto a baking sheet.
4. Place baking sheet on the wire rack, then place the rack at mid-position in the toaster oven.
5. Select the bake mode and set the time to 15 minutes. Press starts.
6. Serve and enjoy.

Nutritional Value (Amount per Serving):

- Calories 110
- Fat 7.4 g
- Carbohydrates 10.6 g
- Sugar 2.6 g
- Protein 3.9 g
- Cholesterol 0 mg

Easy Pumpkin Soup

Preparation Time: 10 minutes

Cooking Time: 8 hours

Serve: 4

Ingredients:

- 2 cups pumpkin puree
- 1/4 tsp ground nutmeg
- 1 cup coconut milk
- 4 cups water
- 1 onion, minced
- 1/4 tsp garlic powder

Directions:

1. Add all ingredients into the pot and stir well to combine. Cover pot with foil.
2. Place pot on the wire rack then places the rack at a low position in the toaster oven.
3. Select the slow cook mode and set the time to 8 hours. Press starts.
4. Puree the soup using a blender until smooth.
5. Stir well and serve.

Nutritional Value (Amount per Serving):

- Calories 66
- Fat 1.4 g
- Carbohydrates 13.1 g
- Sugar 5.3 g
- Protein 1.7 g
- Cholesterol 0 mg

Healthy Cauliflower Soup

Preparation Time: 10 minutes
Cooking Time: 6 hours
Serve: 2

Ingredients:

- 1/2 lb cauliflower florets
- 1 garlic clove, minced
- 1/2 onion, minced
- 1 1/2 tsp curry powder
- 1 1/4 cup chicken stock

Directions:

1. Add all ingredients into the pot and stir well to combine. Cover pot with foil.
2. Place pot on the wire rack then places the rack at a low position in the toaster oven.
3. Select the slow cook mode and set the time to 6 hours. Press starts.
4. Puree the soup using a blender until smooth.
5. Stir well and serve.

Nutritional Value (Amount per Serving):

- Calories 45
- Fat 0.4 g
- Carbohydrates 10 g
- Sugar 4 g
- Protein 2.8 g
- Cholesterol 0 mg

Tasty Sweet Potatoes

Preparation Time: 10 minutes

Cooking Time: 40 minutes

Serve: 4

Ingredients:

- 2 large, sweet potatoes, cut into 1-inch cubes
- 1/2 tsp garlic powder
- 1/2 tsp cumin
- 1/2 tsp chili powder
- 3/4 tsp paprika
- 1 tbsp olive oil
- 1/4 tsp onion powder
- 1/4 tsp pepper
- 1/2 tsp salt

Directions:

1. Preheat the cosori air fryer toaster oven to 400 F.
2. Line baking sheet with parchment paper and set aside.
3. In a bowl, toss sweet potatoes with remaining ingredients until well coated.
4. Spread sweet potatoes onto a baking sheet.
5. Place baking sheet on the wire rack, then place the rack at mid-position in the toaster oven.
6. Select the bake mode and set the time to 40 minutes. Press starts.
7. Serve and enjoy.

Nutritional Value (Amount per Serving):

- Calories 95
- Fat 3.8 g
- Carbohydrates 14.9 g
- Sugar 0.5 g
- Protein 1 g
- Cholesterol 0 mg

Garlic Baby Potatoes

Preparation Time: 10 minutes
Cooking Time: 25 minutes
Serve: 4

Ingredients:

- 1 lb baby potatoes, cut into pieces
- 1 tbsp parsley, chopped
- 1/8 cup feta cheese, crumbled
- 1 tsp thyme, chopped
- 2 garlic cloves, minced
- 1 tbsp olive oil
- Pepper
- Salt

Directions:

1. Preheat the cosori air fryer toaster oven to 400 F.
2. Toss potatoes with thyme, garlic, oil, pepper, and salt.
3. Spread potatoes onto the baking sheet.
4. Place baking sheet on the wire rack, then place the rack at mid-position in the toaster oven.
5. Select the bake mode and set the time to 25 minutes. Press starts.
6. Top with cheese and serve.

Nutritional Value (Amount per Serving):

- Calories 112
- Fat 4.7 g
- Carbohydrates 15 g
- Sugar 0.2 g
- Protein 3.7 g
- Cholesterol 4 mg

Parmesan Squash

Preparation Time: 10 minutes
Cooking Time: 30 minutes
Serve: 6

Ingredients:

- 2 lbs summer squash, cut into 1/4-inch slices
- 1/4 cup olive oil
- 1/2 cup parmesan cheese, grated
- 1/4 cup almond flour
- 1/4 tsp pepper
- 1/2 tsp salt

Directions:

1. Preheat the cosori air fryer toaster oven to 350 F.
2. Add squash slices into the bowl and toss with oil.
3. In a small bowl, mix almond flour, cheese, pepper, and salt.
4. Arrange squash slices into the baking dish and sprinkle with almond flour mixture.
5. Place baking dish on the wire rack, then place the rack at mid-position in the toaster oven.
6. Select the bake mode and set the time to 30 minutes. Press starts.
7. Serve and enjoy.

Nutritional Value (Amount per Serving):

- Calories 153
- Fat 12.6 g
- Carbohydrates 7.2 g
- Sugar 5.3 g
- Protein 4.9 g
- Cholesterol 5 mg

Delicious Turnip Gratin

Preparation Time: 10 minutes
Cooking Time: 30 minutes
Serve: 6

Ingredients:

- 1 1/2 lbs turnip, peel, and slice
- 1 1/4 cup coconut milk
- 1/2 tsp garlic, minced
- 1/2 onion, sliced
- 1.5 oz butter
- 1/4 cup fresh chives, chopped
- 8 oz cheddar cheese, shredded
- Pepper
- Salt

Directions:

1. Preheat the cosori air fryer toaster oven to 400 F.
2. Spray baking dish with cooking spray.
3. Arrange turnip and onion slices into the baking dish. Season with pepper and salt.
4. Pour milk over turnips and onion slices and sprinkle shredded cheddar cheese on top.
5. Place baking dish on the wire rack, then place the rack at mid-position in the toaster oven.
6. Select the bake mode and set the time to 30 minutes. Press starts.
7. Serve and enjoy.

Nutritional Value (Amount per Serving):

- Calories 355
- Fat 30.3 g
- Carbohydrates 11.6 g
- Sugar 6.6 g
- Protein 11.8 g
- Cholesterol 55 mg

Green Beans & Mushrooms

Preparation Time: 5 minutes

Cooking Time: 30 minutes

Serve: 6

Ingredients:

- 1 lb green beans, cut into pieces
- 1 tbsp balsamic vinegar
- 1 1/2 tbsp olive oil
- 8 oz mushrooms, clean and sliced
- 1/4 cup mozzarella cheese, grated
- Pepper
- Salt

Directions:

1. Preheat the cosori air fryer toaster oven to 450 F.
2. Add mushrooms, beans, oil, vinegar, pepper, and salt into the bowl and toss well.
3. Transfer mushroom bean mixture into the baking dish.
4. Place baking dish on the wire rack, then place the rack at mid-position in the toaster oven.
5. Select the bake mode and set the time to 30 minutes. Press starts.
6. Sprinkle cheese on top and serve.

Nutritional Value (Amount per Serving):

- Calories 60
- Fat 4 g
- Carbohydrates 7 g
- Sugar 2 g
- Protein 2 g
- Cholesterol 0 mg

Baked Mushrooms

Preparation Time: 5 minutes
Cooking Time: 15 minutes
Serve: 4

Ingredients:

- 40 mushrooms, clean
- 1 tbsp garlic, minced
- 1/4 cup olive oil
- 1/4 tsp Italian seasoning
- Pepper
- Salt

Directions:

1. Preheat the cosori air fryer toaster oven to 450 F.
2. Add mushroom, Italian seasoning, oil, garlic, pepper, and salt into the baking dish and mix well.
3. Place baking dish on the wire rack, then place the rack at mid-position in the toaster oven.
4. Select the bake mode and set the time to 15 minutes. Press starts.
5. Serve and enjoy.

Nutritional Value (Amount per Serving):

- Calories 150
- Fat 13.1 g
- Carbohydrates 6.6 g
- Sugar 3.1 g
- Protein 5.8 g
- Cholesterol 0 mg

Chapter 7: Snack & Appetizers

Creamy Crab Dip

Preparation Time: 10 minutes

Cooking Time: 20 minutes

Serve: 8

Ingredients:

- 1/2 cup mozzarella cheese, shredded
- 1/2 cup cheddar cheese, shredded
- 1/2 tsp garlic powder
- 12 oz can crab meat, drained
- 1/4 cup mayonnaise
- 1 tsp salt

Directions:

1. Preheat the cosori air fryer toaster oven to 350 F.
2. In a bowl, mix cream cheese, cheddar cheese, garlic powder, crabmeat, mayonnaise, and salt until well combined.
3. Add cream cheese mixture into the greased baking dish and top with mozzarella cheese.
4. Place baking dish on the wire rack, then place the rack at mid-position in the toaster oven.
5. Select the bake mode and set the time to 20 minutes. Press starts.
6. Serve and enjoy.

Nutritional Value (Amount per Serving):

- Calories 85
- Fat 5.1 g
- Carbohydrates 2.8 g
- Sugar 1.3 g
- Protein 7.6 g
- Cholesterol 48 mg

Simple Baked Brie

Preparation Time: 10 minutes
Cooking Time: 15 minutes
Serve: 8

Ingredients:

- 16 oz brie
- 1 tbsp maple syrup
- 2 tbsp almonds, chopped
- 1/4 cup apricot jam
- Pinch of salt

Directions:

1. Preheat the cosori air fryer toaster oven to 400 F.
2. Place brie into the baking dish. Spread apricot jam over brie and sprinkle with almonds.
3. Drizzle with maple syrup and sprinkle with a pinch of salt.
4. Place baking dish on the wire rack, then place the rack at mid-position in the toaster oven.
5. Select the bake mode and set the time to 15 minutes. Press starts.
6. Serve and enjoy.

Nutritional Value (Amount per Serving):

- Calories 229
- Fat 16.5 g
- Carbohydrates 8.7 g
- Sugar 6.2 g
- Protein 12.2 g
- Cholesterol 57 mg

Sweet Onion Dip

Preparation Time: 10 minutes
Cooking Time: 25 minutes
Serve: 10

Ingredients:

- 10 oz sweet onion, peel & slice
- 1 cup cheddar cheese, shredded
- 1/2 cup mozzarella cheese, shredded
- 1/2 cup parmesan cheese, shredded
- 1 cup sour cream
- 1 cup mayonnaise
- 1/4 tsp pepper
- 3/4 tsp salt

Directions:

1. Preheat the cosori air fryer toaster oven to 375 F.
2. Add all ingredients into the bowl and mix until well combined.
3. Pour mixture into the casserole dish.
4. Place casserole dish on the wire rack, then place the rack at mid-position in the toaster oven.
5. Select the bake mode and set the time to 25 minutes. Press starts.
6. Serve and enjoy.

Nutritional Value (Amount per Serving):

- Calories 216
- Fat 17.7 g
- Carbohydrates 9.6 g
- Sugar 2.8 g
- Protein 5.9 g
- Cholesterol 32 mg

Simple Ricotta Cheese Dip

Preparation Time: 10 minutes
Cooking Time: 20 minutes
Serve: 6

Ingredients:

- 2 cups ricotta cheese
- 1 tsp garlic, minced
- 1 lemon zest
- 1/4 cup parmesan cheese, shredded
- 1/2 cup mozzarella cheese, shredded
- Pepper
- Salt

Directions:

1. Preheat the cosori air fryer toaster oven to 375 F.
2. Add all ingredients into the bowl and mix until well combined.
3. Pour mixture into the casserole dish.
4. Place casserole dish on the wire rack, then place the rack at mid-position in the toaster oven.
5. Select the bake mode and set the time to 20 minutes. Press starts.
6. Serve and enjoy.

Nutritional Value (Amount per Serving):

- Calories 128
- Fat 7.2 g
- Carbohydrates 5.4 g
- Sugar 0.5 g
- Protein 10.6 g
- Cholesterol 28 mg

Tender & Juicy Meatballs

Preparation Time: 10 minutes

Cooking Time: 20 minutes

Serve: 6

Ingredients:

- 1 egg
- 1 lb ground beef
- 1 tbsp basil, chopped
- 1 tbsp rosemary, chopped
- 2 tbsp hot sauce
- 1/2 small onion, minced
- 1 tsp garlic, minced
- 1/4 cup parmesan cheese, grated
- 1/2 cup breadcrumbs
- Pepper
- Salt

Directions:

1. Preheat the cosori air fryer toaster oven to 375 F.
2. Line baking sheet with parchment paper and set aside.
3. Add all ingredients into the bowl and mix until well combined.
4. Make small balls from the meat mixture and place them on a baking sheet.
5. Place baking sheet on the wire rack, then place the rack at mid-position in the toaster oven.
6. Select the bake mode and set the time to 20 minutes. Press starts.
7. Serve and enjoy.

Nutritional Value (Amount per Serving):

- Calories 204
- Fat 6.9 g
- Carbohydrates 7.8 g
- Sugar 0.9 g
- Protein 26.4 g
- Cholesterol 98 mg

Perfectly Roasted Almonds

Preparation Time: 10 minutes

Cooking Time: 15 minutes

Serve: 2

Ingredients:

- 1 cup almonds
- 1 tsp liquid smoke
- 1 1/2 tbsp maple syrup
- 1/2 tsp garlic powder
- 1/2 tsp cayenne
- 1/4 tsp pepper
- 1 tsp paprika
- 1 tsp chili powder
- 3/4 tsp salt

Directions:

1. Preheat the cosori air fryer toaster oven to 375 F.
2. Line baking sheet with parchment paper and set aside.
3. Add almonds and remaining ingredients into the bowl and toss well.
4. Spread almonds onto the baking sheet.
5. Place baking sheet on the wire rack, then place the rack at mid-position in the toaster oven.
6. Select the bake mode and set the time to 15 minutes. Press starts.
7. Serve and enjoy.

Nutritional Value (Amount per Serving):

- Calories 325
- Fat 24.2 g
- Carbohydrates 22.5 g
- Sugar 11.4 g
- Protein 10.6 g
- Cholesterol 0 mg

Savory Cashews

Preparation Time: 10 minutes
Cooking Time: 10 minutes
Serve: 4

Ingredients:

- 15 oz cashews
- 2 tbsp everything bagel seasoning
- 1 tbsp olive oil
- Pepper
- Salt

Directions:

1. Preheat the cosori air fryer toaster oven to 350 F.
2. Line baking sheet with parchment paper and set aside.
3. Add cashews and remaining ingredients into the bowl and toss well.
4. Spread cashews onto the baking sheet.
5. Place baking sheet on the wire rack, then place the rack at mid-position in the toaster oven.
6. Select the bake mode and set the time to 10 minutes. Press starts.
7. Serve and enjoy.

Nutritional Value (Amount per Serving):

- Calories 698
- Fat 53 g
- Carbohydrates 46.8 g
- Sugar 6.3 g
- Protein 18.3 g
- Cholesterol 0 mg

Crispy Baked Broccoli

Preparation Time: 10 minutes
Cooking Time: 25 minutes
Serve: 6

Ingredients:

- 3 eggs
- 4 cups broccoli florets
- 1 tsp garlic powder
- 1 tbsp milk
- 1/4 cup parmesan cheese, grated
- 1 cup cheddar cheese, grated
- 1 cup breadcrumbs
- Pepper
- Salt

Directions:

1. Preheat the cosori air fryer toaster oven to 400 F.
2. Line baking sheet with parchment paper and set aside.
3. In a small bowl, whisk eggs with milk, pepper, and salt.
4. In a shallow dish, mix parmesan cheese, cheddar cheese, breadcrumbs, and garlic powder.
5. Dip broccoli florets in egg mixture then coat with parmesan cheese mixture.
6. Place coated broccoli florets onto the parchment paper.
7. Place baking sheet on the wire rack, then place the rack at mid-position in the toaster oven.
8. Select the bake mode and set the time to 25 minutes. Press starts.
9. Serve and enjoy.

Nutritional Value (Amount per Serving):

- Calories 214
- Fat 10.4 g
- Carbohydrates 18 g
- Sugar 2.6 g
- Protein 12.9 g
- Cholesterol 105 mg

Crispy Broccoli Tots

Preparation Time: 10 minutes

Cooking Time: 25 minutes

Serve: 6

Ingredients:

- 1 egg
- 2 tbsp almond flour
- 2 cups cheddar cheese, shredded
- 2 cups broccoli rice, cooked & squeezed out excess liquid
- 1/4 tsp garlic powder
- Pepper
- Salt

Directions:

1. Preheat the cosori air fryer toaster oven to 400 F.
2. Line baking sheet with parchment paper and set aside.
3. Add all ingredients into the bowl and mix until well combined.
4. Make small tots from the mixture and place them on a baking sheet.
5. Place baking sheet on the wire rack, then place the rack at mid-position in the toaster oven.
6. Select the bake mode and set the time to 25 minutes. Press starts.
7. Turn broccoli tots after 15 minutes.
8. Serve and enjoy.

Nutritional Value (Amount per Serving):

- Calories 237
- Fat 14.7 g
- Carbohydrates 14.5 g
- Sugar 1 g
- Protein 12.8 g
- Cholesterol 67 mg

Easy Zucchini Fritters

Preparation Time: 10 minutes

Cooking Time: 20 minutes

Serve: 4

Ingredients:

- 1 egg
- 2 zucchinis, shredded
- 1 tsp garlic powder
- 2 tbsp chives, chopped
- 1/4 cup parmesan cheese, grated
- 1/2 cup cheddar cheese, shredded
- 1 1/4 cup breadcrumbs
- 1 tsp kosher salt

Directions:

1. Preheat the cosori air fryer toaster oven to 375 F.
2. Line baking sheet with parchment paper and set aside.
3. Add all ingredients into the bowl and mix until well combined.
4. Make small patties from the mixture and place them on a baking sheet.
5. Place baking sheet on the wire rack, then place the rack at mid-position in the toaster oven.
6. Select the bake mode and set the time to 20-25 minutes. Press starts.
7. Serve and enjoy.

Nutritional Value (Amount per Serving):

- Calories 230
- Fat 8.1 g
- Carbohydrates 28.5 g
- Sugar 4.1 g
- Protein 11.3 g
- Cholesterol 57 mg

Crispy Potato Wedges

Preparation Time: 10 minutes
Cooking Time: 15 minutes
Serve: 4

Ingredients:

- 2 medium potatoes, cut into wedges
- 1/8 tsp cayenne
- 1/4 tsp garlic powder
- 1/2 tsp paprika
- 1 1/2 tbsp olive oil
- 1/4 tsp pepper
- 1 tsp sea salt

Directions:

1. Preheat the cosori air fryer toaster oven to 400 F.
2. Add potato wedges and remaining ingredients into the bowl and toss well.
3. Place potato wedges in a fry basket.
4. Place the fry basket on the wire rack, then place the rack at the top position in the toaster oven.
5. Select the air fry mode and set the time to 15 minutes. Press starts.
6. Serve and enjoy.

Nutritional Value (Amount per Serving):

- Calories 120
- Fat 5.4 g
- Carbohydrates 17.1 g
- Sugar 1.3 g
- Protein 1.9 g
- Cholesterol 0 mg

Roasted Cauliflower

Preparation Time: 10 minutes

Cooking Time: 17 minutes

Serve: 2

Ingredients:

- 1/2 cauliflower head, cut into florets
- 2 tbsp parmesan cheese
- 1/3 cup Italian dressing

Directions:

1. Preheat the cosori air fryer toaster oven to 400 F.
2. Add cauliflower florets and Italian dressing into the bowl and toss well.
3. Place cauliflower florets in a fry basket.
4. Place the fry basket on the wire rack, then place the rack at the top position in the toaster oven.
5. Select the air fry mode and set the time to 10 minutes. Press starts.
6. Sprinkle parmesan cheese over cauliflower florets and air fry for 7 minutes more.
7. Serve and enjoy.

Nutritional Value (Amount per Serving):

- Calories 221
- Fat 17.2 g
- Carbohydrates 8.6 g
- Sugar 4.9 g
- Protein 10.5 g
- Cholesterol 46 mg

Crispy Okra

Preparation Time: 10 minutes
Cooking Time: 15 minutes
Serve: 4

Ingredients:

- 12 oz okra, cut into 1/4-inch-thick rounds
- 2 tsp olive oil
- 1 tsp old bay seasoning
- 2 tbsp cornmeal
- 2 tbsp flour

Directions:

1. Preheat the cosori air fryer toaster oven to 400 F.
2. Add okra and remaining ingredients into the bowl and toss well.
3. Place okra in the fry basket.
4. Place the fry basket on the wire rack, then place the rack at the top position in the toaster oven.
5. Select the air fry mode and set the time to 15 minutes. Press starts.
6. Turn okra after 10 minutes.
7. Serve and enjoy.

Nutritional Value (Amount per Serving):

- Calories 82
- Fat 2.7 g
- Carbohydrates 12.3 g
- Sugar 1.3 g
- Protein 2.4 g
- Cholesterol 0 mg

Healthy Beet Chips

Preparation Time: 10 minutes
Cooking Time: 15 minutes
Serve: 2

Ingredients:

- 2 beetroots, peel & slice
- 1/2 tbsp olive oil
- Pepper
- Salt

Directions:

1. Preheat the cosori air fryer toaster oven to 400 F.
2. Add beet slices, oil, pepper, and salt into the bowl and toss well.
3. Place beet slices in a fry basket.
4. Place the fry basket on the wire rack, then place the rack at the top position in the toaster oven.
5. Select the air fry mode and set the time to 15 minutes. Press starts.
6. Serve and enjoy.

Nutritional Value (Amount per Serving):

- Calories 65
- Fat 3.5 g
- Carbohydrates 8 g
- Sugar 5 g
- Protein 1 g
- Cholesterol 0 mg

Corn Zucchini Fritters

Preparation Time: 10 minutes

Cooking Time: 12 minutes

Serve: 4

Ingredients:

- 2 zucchini, grated & squeezed
- 2 garlic cloves, minced
- 2 tbsp chickpea flour
- 1 potato, cooked & grated
- 1 cup corn kernels
- Pepper
- Salt

Directions:

1. Preheat the cosori air fryer toaster oven to 360 F.
2. Add all ingredients into the bowl and toss well.
3. Make small patties from the mixture and place in a fry basket.
4. Place the fry basket on the wire rack, then place the rack at the top position in the toaster oven.
5. Select the air fry mode and set the time to 12 minutes. Press starts.
6. Turn patties after 8 minutes.
7. Serve and enjoy.

Nutritional Value (Amount per Serving):

- Calories 106
- Fat 1.1 g
- Carbohydrates 22.3 g
- Sugar 4 g
- Protein 4.6 g
- Cholesterol 0 mg

Chapter 8: Dehydrate

Dried Mango

Preparation Time: 10 minutes
Cooking Time: 4 hours
Serve: 8

Ingredients:

- 4 mangoes, sliced
- 1 tbsp chili powder
- 1/4 cup lime juice
- 1/4 tsp salt

Directions:

1. In a bowl, toss mango slices with chili powder, lime juice, and salt.
2. Arrange mango slices in a fry basket.
3. Place the fry basket on the wire rack, then place the rack at the top mid-position in the toaster oven.
4. Select dehydrate mode. Set temperature to 135 F and time for 4 hours. Press starts.

Nutritional Value (Amount per Serving):

- Calories 104
- Fat 0.8 g
- Carbohydrates 25.8 g
- Sugar 23 g
- Protein 1.5 g
- Cholesterol 0 mg

Dried Pineapple Slices

Preparation Time: 10 minutes
Cooking Time: 16 hours
Serve: 8

Ingredients:

- 1 ripe pineapple, peel, core, & sliced
- 2 tbsp water
- 1/4 tsp cinnamon
- 1/4 cup honey
- 3 tbsp hot sauce

Directions:

1. In a large bowl, add pineapple slices, water, cinnamon, honey, and hot sauce and toss well.
2. Arrange pineapple slices in a fry basket.
3. Place the fry basket on the wire rack, then place the rack at the top mid-position in the toaster oven.
4. Select dehydrate mode. Set temperature to 125 F and time for 16 hours. Press starts.

Nutritional Value (Amount per Serving):

- Calories 43
- Fat 0 g
- Carbohydrates 11.6 g
- Sugar 10.8 g
- Protein 0.2 g
- Cholesterol 0 mg

Dried Cranberries

Preparation Time: 10 minutes

Cooking Time: 20 hours

Serve: 8

Ingredients:

- 3 cups cranberries

Directions:

1. Arrange cranberries in a fry basket.
2. Place the fry basket on the wire rack, then place the rack at the top mid-position in the toaster oven.
3. Select dehydrate mode. Set temperature to 135 F and time for 20 hours. Press starts.

Nutritional Value (Amount per Serving):

- Calories 23
- Fat 0 g
- Carbohydrates 3.8 g
- Sugar 1.5 g
- Protein 0 g
- Cholesterol 0 mg

Dried Pear Slices

Preparation Time: 10 minutes

Cooking Time: 20 hours

Serve: 6

Ingredients:

- 4 pears, cut into 1/4-inch-thick slices

Directions:

1. Arrange pear slices in a fry basket.
2. Place the fry basket on the wire rack, then place the rack at the top mid-position in the toaster oven.
3. Select dehydrate mode. Set temperature to 135 F and time for 20 hours. Press starts.

Nutritional Value (Amount per Serving):

- Calories 81
- Fat 0.2 g
- Carbohydrates 21.2 g
- Sugar 13.6 g
- Protein 0.5 g
- Cholesterol 0 mg

Dried Orange Slices

Preparation Time: 10 minutes

Cooking Time: 8 hours

Serve: 6

Ingredients:

- 4 oranges, cut into 1/4-inch-thick slices

Directions:

1. Arrange orange slices in a fry basket.
2. Place the fry basket on the wire rack, then place the rack at the top mid-position in the toaster oven.
3. Select dehydrate mode. Set temperature to 135 F and time for 8 hours. Press starts.

Nutritional Value (Amount per Serving):

- Calories 58
- Fat 0.2 g
- Carbohydrates 14.4 g
- Sugar 11.5 g
- Protein 1.2 g
- Cholesterol 0 mg

Dried Raspberries

Preparation Time: 10 minutes
Cooking Time: 8 hours
Serve: 4

Ingredients:

- 2 cups raspberries

Directions:

1. Arrange raspberries in a fry basket.
2. Place the fry basket on the wire rack, then place the rack at the top mid-position in the toaster oven.
3. Select dehydrate mode. Set temperature to 135 F and time for 8 hours. Press starts.

Nutritional Value (Amount per Serving):

- Calories 32
- Fat 0.4 g
- Carbohydrates 7.3 g
- Sugar 2.7 g
- Protein 0.7 g
- Cholesterol 0 mg

Apple Chips

Preparation Time: 10 minutes

Cooking Time: 6 hours

Serve: 4

Ingredients:

- 4 apples, cut into 1/4-inch-thick slices
- 1 tbsp cinnamon
- 2 tbsp maple syrup
- 1 tbsp lemon juice

Directions:

1. In a bowl, toss apple slices with cinnamon, maple syrup, and lemon juice.
2. Arrange apple slices in a fry basket.
3. Place the fry basket on the wire rack, then place the rack at the top mid-position in the toaster oven.
4. Select dehydrate mode. Set temperature to 130 F and time for 6 hours. Press starts.

Nutritional Value (Amount per Serving):

- Calories 147
- Fat 0.5 g
- Carbohydrates 39 g
- Sugar 29.3 g
- Protein 0.7 g
- Cholesterol 0 mg

Radish Chips

Preparation Time: 10 minutes

Cooking Time: 5 hours

Serve: 4

Ingredients:

- 4 radishes, cut into 1/8-inch-thick slices
- Salt

Directions:

1. Arrange radish slices in a fry basket and season with salt.
2. Place the fry basket on the wire rack, then place the rack at the top mid-position in the toaster oven.
3. Select dehydrate mode. Set temperature to 125 F and time for 5 hours. Press starts.

Nutritional Value (Amount per Serving):

- Calories 1
- Fat 0 g
- Carbohydrates 0.2 g
- Sugar 0.1 g
- Protein 0 g
- Cholesterol 0 mg

Beet Chips

Preparation Time: 10 minutes
Cooking Time: 6 hours
Serve: 6

Ingredients:

- 4 small beets, cut into 1/4-inch-thick slices
- 1 tbsp olive oil
- 1/2 cup water
- 1/2 cup apple cider vinegar
- Salt

Directions:

1. In a bowl, add beet slices, oil, water, vinegar, and salt, and let it sit for 20 minutes.
2. Drain beet slices and arrange beet slices in a fry basket.
3. Place the fry basket on the wire rack, then place the rack at the top mid-position in the toaster oven.
4. Select dehydrate mode. Set temperature to 125 F and time for 6 hours. Press starts.

Nutritional Value (Amount per Serving):

- Calories 49
- Fat 2.4 g
- Carbohydrates 5.8 g
- Sugar 4.6 g
- Protein 1 g
- Cholesterol 0 mg

Cucumber Chips

Preparation Time: 10 minutes
Cooking Time: 5 hours
Serve: 6

Ingredients:

- 3 cucumbers, thinly sliced
- 1/2 tsp mustard powder
- 1 tbsp paprika
- 1 tsp chili powder
- 1 1/2 tsp garlic salt

Directions:

1. In a bowl, toss cucumber slices with mustard powder, paprika, chili powder, and garlic salt.
2. Arrange cucumber slices in a fry basket.
3. Place the fry basket on the wire rack, then place the rack at the top mid-position in the toaster oven.
4. Select dehydrate mode. Set temperature to 125 F and time for 5 hours. Press starts.

Nutritional Value (Amount per Serving):

- Calories 31
- Fat 0.5 g
- Carbohydrates 7 g
- Sugar 2.9 g
- Protein 1.4 g
- Cholesterol 0 mg

Chapter 9: Desserts

Delicious Chocolate Cupcakes

Preparation Time: 10 minutes
Cooking Time: 16 minutes
Serve: 12

Ingredients:

- 1 egg
- 1/4 cup boiling water
- 1/3 cup buttermilk
- 1 tsp vanilla
- 3/4 cup sugar
- 1/3 cup canola oil
- 1/2 tsp baking soda
- 1/2 tsp baking powder
- 1/2 cup cocoa powder
- 3/4 cup all-purpose flour
- 1/4 tsp salt

Directions:

1. Preheat the cosori air fryer toaster oven to 350 F.
2. Line muffin pan with cupcake liners and set aside.
3. In a bowl, mix together flour, baking powder, baking soda, cocoa powder, and salt.
4. In a separate bowl, beat together egg, sugar, oil, buttermilk, and vanilla.
5. Add flour mixture and mix well. Add boiling water and beat on low speed until well combined.
6. Spoon the batter into the prepared pan.
7. Place muffin pan on the wire rack, then place the rack at mid-position in the toaster oven.
8. Select the bake mode and set the time to 16 minutes. Press starts.
9. Serve and enjoy.

Nutritional Value (Amount per Serving):

- Calories 146
- Fat 7 g
- Carbohydrates 20.9 g
- Sugar 13 g
- Protein 2.2 g
- Cholesterol 14 mg

Moist Lemon Cupcakes

Preparation Time: 10 minutes
Cooking Time: 17 minutes
Serve: 12

Ingredients:

- 2 eggs
- 1/4 cup fresh lemon juice
- 1/4 cup warm milk
- 1/2 cup sour cream
- 3/4 cup butter, melted
- 1 1/2 tsp baking powder
- 1/4 tsp baking soda
- 2 tbsp lemon zest
- 1 cup sugar
- 1 2/3 cup all-purpose flour
- 1/4 tsp kosher salt

Directions:

1. Preheat the cosori air fryer toaster oven to 375 F.
2. Line muffin pan with cupcake liners and set aside.
3. Add lemon zest and sugar to the food processor and process until sugar is pale yellow in color.
4. In a large bowl, mix flour, baking powder, baking soda, and salt and set aside.
5. In a separate bowl, whisk eggs, sugar, sour cream, lemon juice, and butter until well combined.
6. Pour egg mixture into the flour mixture and mix until well combined.
7. Spoon batter into the prepared pan.
8. Place muffin pan on the wire rack, then place the rack at mid-position in the toaster oven.
9. Select the bake mode and set the time to 17 minutes. Press starts.
10. Serve and enjoy.

Nutritional Value (Amount per Serving):

- Calories 263
- Fat 14.6 g
- Carbohydrates 31.3 g
- Sugar 17.2 g
- Protein 3.4 g
- Cholesterol 62 mg

Classic Carrot Cake

Preparation Time: 10 minutes
Cooking Time: 30 minutes
Serve: 12

Ingredients:

- 4 eggs
- 1/2 cups walnuts, chopped
- 1 1/2 tsp cinnamon
- 1 1/2 tsp vanilla
- 1 tsp baking powder
- 1 cup canola oil
- 2 cups flour
- 3 cups carrots, grated
- 2 cups sugar

Directions:

1. Preheat the cosori air fryer toaster oven to 350 F.
2. Spray cakes pan with cooking spray and set aside.
3. In a bowl, beat eggs and sugar at low speed for 5 minutes.
4. Add flour, cinnamon, and baking powder and mix for 2 minutes.
5. Add walnuts and carrots and stir well.
6. Pour batter into the prepared cake pan.
7. Place cakes pan on the wire rack, then place the rack at mid-position in the toaster oven.
8. Select the bake mode and set the time to 30 minutes. Press starts.
9. Slice and serve.

Nutritional Value (Amount per Serving):

- Calories 429
- Fat 22.9 g
- Carbohydrates 53.1 g
- Sugar 35 g
- Protein 5.5 g
- Cholesterol 55 mg

Easy Vanilla Cake

Preparation Time: 10 minutes
Cooking Time: 30 minutes
Serve: 8

Ingredients:

- 2 eggs
- 1 tsp orange extract
- 1/4 cup milk
- 1 tsp baking powder
- 1/3 cup sugar
- 1/3 cup canola oil
- 1 cup all-purpose flour

Directions:

1. Preheat the cosori air fryer toaster oven to 350 F.
2. In a bowl, mix flour, sugar, and baking powder and set aside.
3. In a separate bowl, whisk eggs with milk. Add oil and orange extract and whisk until light.
4. Add flour mixture into the egg mixture and mix until well combined.
5. Pour batter into the greased loaf pan.
6. Place loaf pan on the wire rack, then place the rack at mid-position in the toaster oven.
7. Select the bake mode and set the time to 30 minutes. Press starts.
8. Slice and serve.

Nutritional Value (Amount per Serving):

- Calories 190
- Fat 10.5 g
- Carbohydrates 21.1 g
- Sugar 8.9 g
- Protein 3.2 g
- Cholesterol 42 mg

Healthy Apple Oat Bars

Preparation Time: 10 minutes

Cooking Time: 25 minutes

Serve: 16

Ingredients:

- 1 cup rolled oats
- 1 cup applesauce
- 1 cup quick oats
- 2 tbsp maple syrup
- 2 tbsp butter, melted
- 1 tsp cinnamon
- 2 tbsp chia seeds

Directions:

1. Preheat the cosori air fryer toaster oven to 375 F.
2. Line square cake tin with parchment paper and set aside.
3. In a bowl, mix oats, cinnamon, and chia seeds. Add applesauce, maple syrup, and butter and mix until well combined.
4. Pour batter into the prepared cake tin.
5. Place cake tin on the wire rack, then place the rack at mid-position in the toaster oven.
6. Select the bake mode and set the time to 25 minutes. Press starts.
7. Slice and serve.

Nutritional Value (Amount per Serving):

- Calories 83
- Fat 3.2 g
- Carbohydrates 12 g
- Sugar 3.2 g
- Protein 2 g
- Cholesterol 4 mg

Cashew Blondies

Preparation Time: 10 minutes

Cooking Time: 40 minutes

Serve: 16

Ingredients:

- 2 eggs
- 1 cup cashews, roasted & chopped
- 1 tbsp vanilla
- 2 cups brown sugar
- 1 cup butter, softened
- 1 tsp baking powder
- 1 1/2 cups all-purpose flour
- 1 tsp salt

Directions:

1. Preheat the cosori air fryer toaster oven to 350 F.
2. Grease an 8-inch baking pan and set it aside.
3. In a bowl, mix flour, salt, and baking powder and set aside.
4. In a bowl, beat butter and sugar until smooth. Add eggs and vanilla and beat until well combined.
5. Slowly add flour mixture and mix until well combined. Add cashews and stir well.
6. Pour batter into the prepared pan and spread evenly.
7. Place baking pan on the wire rack, then place the rack at mid-position in the toaster oven.
8. Select the bake mode and set the time to 40 minutes. Press starts.
9. Slice and serve.

Nutritional Value (Amount per Serving):

- Calories 273
- Fat 16.1 g
- Carbohydrates 29.8 g
- Sugar 18.2 g
- Protein 3.4 g
- Cholesterol 51 mg

Chewy Brownies

Preparation Time: 10 minutes
Cooking Time: 25 minutes
Serve: 12

Ingredients:

- 3 eggs
- 1/4 tsp baking powder
- 1/3 cup cocoa powder
- 3/4 cup flour
- 1 1/2 tsp vanilla
- 1 1/2 cups sugar
- 3/4 cup canola oil
- 1/4 tsp salt

Directions:

1. Preheat the cosori air fryer toaster oven to 350 F.
2. Grease 9*9-inch baking pan and set aside.
3. In a bowl, mix oil, vanilla, and sugar. Add eggs and whisk until well combined.
4. Mix flour, baking powder, cocoa powder, and salt.
5. Slowly add flour mixture into the egg mixture and mix until well combined.
6. Pour batter into the prepared baking pan.
7. Place baking pan on the wire rack, then place the rack at mid-position in the toaster oven.
8. Select the bake mode and set the time to 25 minutes. Press starts.
9. Slice and serve.

Nutritional Value (Amount per Serving):

- Calories 265
- Fat 15.1 g
- Carbohydrates 32.5 g
- Sugar 25.2 g
- Protein 2.6 g
- Cholesterol 41 mg

Soft Baked Donuts

Preparation Time: 10 minutes
Cooking Time: 10 minutes
Serve: 12

Ingredients:

- 2 eggs
- 1 tsp vanilla
- 2 tbsp canola oil
- 3/4 cup buttermilk
- 1/2 tsp ground nutmeg
- 1/2 tsp cinnamon
- 2 tsp baking powder
- 3/4 cup sugar
- 2 cups all-purpose flour
- 1/2 tsp salt

Directions:

1. Preheat the cosori air fryer toaster oven to 425 F.
2. Spray donuts pan with cooking spray and set aside.
3. In a bowl, mix flour, nutmeg, cinnamon, baking powder, sugar, and salt.
4. In a separate bowl, whisk eggs with vanilla, oil, and buttermilk.
5. Pour egg mixture into the flour mixture and mix until well combined.
6. Pour batter into the prepared donut pan.
7. Place the donut pan on the wire rack, then place the rack at mid-position in the toaster oven.
8. Select the bake mode and set the time to 10 minutes. Press starts.
9. Serve and enjoy.

Nutritional Value (Amount per Serving):

- Calories 162
- Fat 3.4 g
- Carbohydrates 29.7 g
- Sugar 13.4 g
- Protein 3.6 g
- Cholesterol 28 mg

Delicious Apple Cake

Preparation Time: 10 minutes
Cooking Time: 35 minutes
Serve: 8

Ingredients:

- 3 eggs
- 1/4 oz chocolate, grated
- 1/2 cup walnuts, chopped
- 1/2 cup pecans, chopped
- 3 cups apples, chopped
- 1 1/2 tsp cinnamon
- 1 tsp baking soda
- 2 cups all-purpose flour
- 3/4 cup canola oil
- 1 1/2 cups sugar

Directions:

1. Preheat the cosori air fryer toaster oven to 350 F.
2. In a bowl, beat eggs, oil, cinnamon, baking soda, flour, and sugar.
3. Add apple, nuts, and chocolate and stir well.
4. Pour batter into the greased 9*13-inch cake pan.
5. Place cakes pan on the wire rack, then place the rack at mid-position in the toaster oven.
6. Select the bake mode and set the time to 35 minutes. Press starts.
7. Slice and serve.

Nutritional Value (Amount per Serving):

- Calories 562
- Fat 28.1 g
- Carbohydrates 74.8 g
- Sugar 47 g
- Protein 7.6 g
- Cholesterol 62 mg

Easy Lemon Muffins

Preparation Time: 10 minutes
Cooking Time: 20 minutes
Serve: 12

Ingredients:

- 1 egg
- 1 cup ricotta cheese
- 1 tsp lemon extract
- 1 tbsp lemon juice
- 1 tbsp lemon zest, grated
- 1/2 cup butter, softened
- 1 cup sugar
- 1/2 tsp baking soda
- 1/2 tsp baking powder
- 2 cups all-purpose flour
- 1/2 tsp salt

Directions:

1. Preheat the cosori air fryer toaster oven to 350 F.
2. Line muffin pan with cupcake liners and set aside.
3. In a bowl, beat egg, butter, and sugar. Add lemon extract, lemon juice, lemon zest, and ricotta cheese and mix well.
4. In a separate bowl, mix flour, baking soda, baking powder, and salt.
5. Add flour mixture into the egg mixture and mix until well combined.
6. Spoon batter into the prepared muffin pan.
7. Place muffin pan on the wire rack, then place the rack at mid-position in the toaster oven.
8. Select the bake mode and set the time to 20 minutes. Press starts.
9. Serve and enjoy.

Nutritional Value (Amount per Serving):

- Calories 242
- Fat 9.9 g
- Carbohydrates 33.9 g
- Sugar 16.9 g
- Protein 5.1 g
- Cholesterol 40 mg

Chapter 10: 30-Day Meal Plan

Day 1

Breakfast- Sausage Casserole Omelet

Lunch- Delicious Chicken with Mushrooms

Dinner- Flavorful Beef Chili

Day 2

Breakfast- Healthy Baked Oatmeal

Lunch- Garlic Butter Shrimp

Dinner- Delicious Beef Barbacoa

Day 3

Breakfast- Sausage Hash brown Casserole

Lunch- Tasty Chicken Casserole

Dinner- Flavorful Halibut

Day 4

Breakfast- Easy Cheesy Breakfast Casserole

Lunch- Curried Fish Fillets

Dinner- Italian Beef Roast

Day 5

Breakfast- Ham Bacon Breakfast Casserole

Lunch- Flavorful Chicken Stew

Dinner- Delicious Catfish Fillets

Day 6

Breakfast- Healthy Baked Frittata

Lunch- Crispy Shrimp

Dinner- Rosemary Lemon Lamb Roast

Day 7

Breakfast- Zucchini Egg Bake

Lunch- Lemon Chicken

Dinner- Lemon Pepper Fish Fillets

Day 8

Breakfast- Spicy Egg Muffins

Lunch- Salmon with Carrots

Dinner- Flavors Pork Cacciatore

Day 9

Breakfast- Pumpkin Pie Oatmeal

Lunch- Pepper Artichoke Chicken

Dinner- Baked Lemon Cod

Day 10

Breakfast- Mushroom Asparagus Egg Bake

Lunch- Herb Salmon

Dinner- Greek Pork Roast

Day 11

Breakfast- Broccoli Egg Bake

Lunch- Tasty Chili Chicken

Dinner- Baked Tilapia with Feta Cheese

Day 12

Breakfast- Cheddar Kale Egg Cups

Lunch- Lemon White Fish Fillets

Dinner- Salsa Pork

Day 13

Breakfast- Artichoke Spinach Bake

Lunch- Simple Turkey Breast

Dinner- Italian Salmon

Day 14

Breakfast- Hash brown Mushroom Casserole

Lunch- Greek Salmon

Dinner- Garlic Beef Roast

Day 15

Breakfast- Broccoli Egg Bake

Lunch- Italian Chicken

Dinner- Greek Pork Roast

Day 16

Breakfast- Sausage Casserole Omelet

Lunch- Delicious Chicken with Mushrooms

Dinner- Flavorful Beef Chili

Day 17

Breakfast- Healthy Baked Oatmeal

Lunch- Garlic Butter Shrimp

Dinner- Delicious Beef Barbacoa

Day 18

Breakfast- Sausage Hash brown Casserole

Lunch- Tasty Chicken Casserole

Dinner- Flavorful Halibut

Day 19

Breakfast- Easy Cheesy Breakfast Casserole

Lunch- Curried Fish Fillets

Dinner- Italian Beef Roast

Day 20

Breakfast- Ham Bacon Breakfast Casserole

Lunch- Flavorful Chicken Stew

Dinner- Delicious Catfish Fillets

Day 21

Breakfast- Healthy Baked Frittata

Lunch- Crispy Shrimp

Dinner- Rosemary Lemon Lamb Roast

Day 22

Breakfast- Zucchini Egg Bake

Lunch- Lemon Chicken

Dinner- Lemon Pepper Fish Fillets

Day 23

Breakfast- Spicy Egg Muffins

Lunch- Salmon with Carrots

Dinner- Flavors Pork Cacciatore

Day 24

Breakfast- Pumpkin Pie Oatmeal

Lunch- Pepper Artichoke Chicken

Dinner- Baked Lemon Cod

Day 25

Breakfast- Mushroom Asparagus Egg Bake

Lunch- Herb Salmon

Dinner- Greek Pork Roast

Day 26

Breakfast- Broccoli Egg Bake

Lunch- Tasty Chili Chicken

Dinner- Baked Tilapia with Feta Cheese

Day 27

Breakfast- Cheddar Kale Egg Cups

Lunch- Lemon White Fish Fillets

Dinner- Salsa Pork

Day 28

Breakfast- Artichoke Spinach Bake

Lunch- Simple Turkey Breast

Dinner- Italian Salmon

Day 29

Breakfast- Hash brown Mushroom Casserole

Lunch- Greek Salmon

Dinner- Garlic Beef Roast

Day 30

Breakfast- Broccoli Egg Bake

Lunch- Italian Chicken

Dinner- Greek Pork Roast

Conclusion

The Cosori smart air fryer toaster oven is one of the advanced and innovative cooking appliances manufactured by COSORI. It is a multi-functional 12 in 1 cooking appliance that comes with 12 different cooking operations like Air frying, baking, roasting, toasting, dehydrating, preheating, keep warm, pizza, slow cooking, broiling, defrosting, and fermentation. The font large glass will help to see the cooking process. The oven comes with a big digital display panel with touch control buttons.

This cookbook contains healthy and delicious recipes comes from different categories like breakfast, beef, lamb, pork, poultry, seafood, fish, dehydrate, vegetables, side dishes, desserts, appetizer, and snacks. The recipes written in this book are unique and written into an easily understandable form. All the recipes start with their preparation and cooking time followed by step-by-step cooking instructions. At the end of each recipe, nutritional value information is written. The nutritional value information will help to keep track of daily calorie intake.

Made in the USA
Las Vegas, NV
15 January 2024

84424589R00077